ALL ABOUT
DERIVATIVES
Mathematical Differentiation
for College Students

Abdul Latiff Md Ahood
Mohd Amirul Mahamud

SUNWAY
UNIVERSITY PRESS

Copyright © 2018 by Sunway University Sdn Bhd

Published by Sunway University Press
An imprint of Sunway University Sdn Bhd

No. 5, Jalan Universiti
Sunway City
47500 Selangor Darul Ehsan
Malaysia

press.sunway.edu.my

Perpustakaan Negara Malaysia   Cataloguing-in-Publication Data

Abdul Latiff Md. Ahood
    ALL ABOUT DERIVATIVES / ABDUL LATIFF BIN MD AHOOD,
    MOHD AMIRUL BIN MAHAMUD.
    ISBN 978-967-13697-3-9
    1. Derivatives (Mathematics).   2. Mathematics--Study and teaching
    (Higher).   I. Mohd. Amirul Mahamud.   II. Title.
    515.33

Printed and bound by CPI Group (UK) Ltd, Croydon, CR0 4YY

Cover image: Studiojumpee/Shutterstock.com
Image used under license from Shutterstock.com

"This book is dedicated to my wife, Nasrah Hanum, and daughter, Fairuz Hanim, who have always been a source of encouragement and inspiration to me."

Abdul Latiff Md Ahood

CONTENTS

LIST OF GRAPHS

LIST OF ACRONYMS AND ABBREVIATIONS

–ve   Negative

+ve   Positive

LHS   Left Hand Side

RHS   Right Hand Side

ABOUT THE AUTHORS

Abdul Latiff Md Ahood is an accomplished lecturer whose teaching career in tertiary education spans over more than 40 years. A respected educator in Electrical Engineering and Mathematics, he has authored several books including *Mesin Elektrik* and *Let's Talk Mathematics*. His knowledge and experience landed him prominent positions in higher education institutions, such as Deputy Dean of the School of Applied Sciences at Universiti Sains Malaysia and Associate Professor at Universiti Teknikal Malaysia Melaka. He is currently teaching Mathematics Unit 1 in the Monash University Foundation Year programme at Sunway College in the capacity of Senior Lecturer.

Mohd Amirul Mahamud is the author of several journal publications and the co-author of *Let's Talk Mathematics*. He has accumulated almost 10 years of experience in education as Lecturer, teaching Algebra and Calculus in various post-secondary courses, and played a crucial role in restructuring the Mathematics syllabus at Albukhary International University. His areas of expertise include, but are not limited to, Pure Mathematics, Mathematical Analysis, Algebraic Geometry and Differential Algebra.

PREFACE

All About Derivatives explains the techniques of differentiating all types of mathematical functions, ranging from polynomials to exponential and logarithmic functions. The basic principles are carefully explained and comprehensively illustrated with numerous worked examples taken from lectures presented over the years.

This book has been written specially to cater to students studying Foundation or Matriculation Mathematics at tertiary level. Some of the advanced problems posed in the book, such as those concerned with partial derivatives and implicit differentiation, might even require students to carry out research beyond the scope of the syllabus.

However, every effort has been made to account for all the differentiation steps without skipping the fundamental concepts. The rigorous worked examples and problem sets found in every chapter will further help test and develop students' skills and understanding.

We genuinely hope that our book will help students grasp the fundamental concepts of Calculus and improve their analytical and critical-thinking skills.

Abdul Latiff Md Ahood
Mohd Amirul Mahamud

FOREWORD

All About Derivatives discusses the concepts and techniques of differentiation of all kinds of functions, ranging from polynomials to exponential and logarithmic functions. In this practical handbook, all the essential principles are explained and demonstrated with complete worked examples. It has been written with the intention to provide study materials and guidelines in such a way that readers would feel guided by a teacher while exploring the book themselves.

The worked examples provided, along with the problem sets at the end of each chapter, run the gamut from fundamental questions to more advanced ones. These have been meticulously prepared to enhance problem-solving skills and encourage independent learning. Students will tackle problems that are related to applications in real life instead of deliberating about limits and continuity, and this makes for a practical guide for students, especially those majoring in Engineering.

Efforts made by the writers to account for all the steps in the worked examples are well-intended, as this will ensure that readers are not only able to understand and work out all the problem sets provided in the book, but are also able to solve problems that they will encounter in the future. The book is suitable for students who are taking Mathematics at diploma level, as well as for foundation students preparing to undergo higher level of studies in Sciences, Technology, Engineering, and Mathematics (STEM)-related fields.

Dr Hailiza Kamarulhaili
Dean and Professor
School of Mathematics
Universiti Sains Malaysia (USM)

ACKNOWLEDGEMENTS

This book would not have been possible without the support of many individuals.

First, we would like to recognise the numerous students in our courses whom we have enjoyed teaching over the years. They have inspired us to produce simplified books to help students learn, understand and appreciate Mathematics.

The support given by the Director of the Monash University Foundation Year programme, Mr Lee Thye Cheong, is most encouraging and has spurred us on to get this book published as soon as possible. Ms Carol Wong, the Head of Sunway University Press, has also played an active role in supporting and facilitating all our efforts.

Most importantly, we would also like to thank our families who constantly encouraged us as we worked on completing this book.

Abdul Latiff Md Ahood
Mohd Amirul Mahamud

CHAPTER 1

DIFFERENTIATION OF POLYNOMIALS

INTRODUCTION

By definition, a straight line is a graph with a constant gradient. For example, the gradient of the straight line $f(x) = 2x$, shown in Figure 1.1, is always the same whether it is measured at a or b.

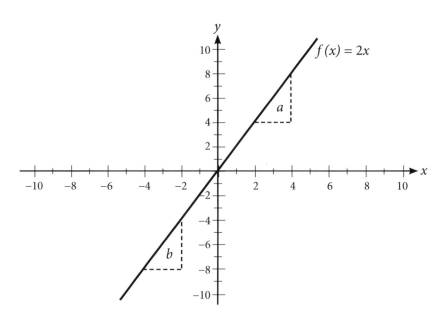

Figure 1.1   Gradient of a straight line

On the other hand, the gradient of the curve $f(x) = x^2 - 2$ changes all the time as you move along the curve. Its gradient varies from point to point as shown in Figure 1.2.

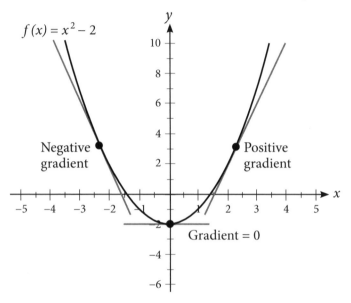

Figure 1.2   Gradient of a curve

The gradient of a polynomial function at any point can be determined by drawing a tangent line at the point. While it is not too difficult to draw the tangent line, a computational method for determining the gradient would, of course, be more convenient and efficient.

 NOTE

A tangent line is not just a straight line that touches the graph at one point, it also acts as the straight line that best approximates the graph at that point.

Let us say that you have a polynomial equation $y = x^2$ and the tangent line drawn at point P_1 as shown in Figure 1.3.

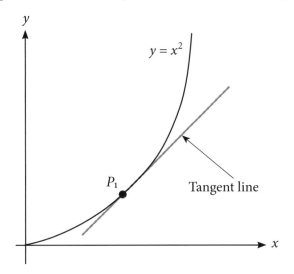

Figure 1.3   Tangent line

From Figure 1.3, the gradient line or tangent line can be moved and adjusted to produce a secant line intersecting the curve at two neighbouring points as shown in Figure 1.4. The transition from the tangent line to the secant line has produced two points, $P_1(x, y)$ and $P_2(x + \delta x, y + \delta y)$, which can be used to help you determine the gradient of the tangent line.

NOTE

The coordinates of P_2 are written as $(x + \delta x, y + \delta y)$ where δx represents a small increment in the value of x and δy is the corresponding increment in the value of y.

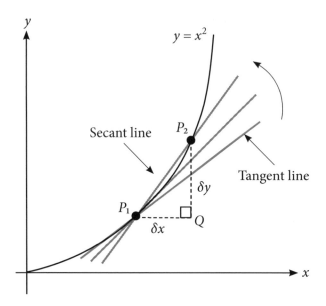

Figure 1.4   Secant line

How is the secant line useful when its gradient is obviously different from the gradient of the tangent line? This is where the idea of 'limits' in differentiation come into the picture. Notice that as you move the secant line back to the position of the original tangent line, point P_2 gets closer and closer to point P_1, which in turn means that both δx and δy approach zero.

Let us consider the polynomial function $y = x^2$. Then, at point P_1, you have

$$y + \delta y = (x + \delta x)^2$$

$$y + \delta y = (x + \delta x)(x + \delta x)$$ •————| Apply the expansion rule

$$y + \delta y = x^2 + x(\delta x) + x(\delta x) + (\delta x)^2$$
$$y + \delta y = x^2 + 2x(\delta x) + (\delta x)^2$$
$$x^2 + \delta y = x^2 + 2x(\delta x) + (\delta x)^2 \quad \bullet\!\!-\!\!\!| \quad y = x^2$$
$$\delta y = x^2 - x^2 + 2x(\delta x) + (\delta x)^2 \quad \bullet\!\!-\!\!| \text{ Bring } x^2 \text{ to the RHS}$$
$$\delta y = 2x(\delta x) + (\delta x)^2 \qquad\qquad \textbf{[Equation 1]}$$

The gradient of the line P_1P_2 can be derived by dividing the change in y with the change in x. Thus, you have

$$\frac{\delta y}{\delta x} = \frac{2x(\delta x) + (\delta x)^2}{\delta x} \quad \bullet\!\!-\!\!\!\!| \begin{array}{l} \text{Divide by } \delta x \\ \text{on both sides} \end{array}$$

$$\frac{\delta y}{\delta x} = \frac{\delta x[2x + \delta x]}{\delta x} \quad \bullet\!\!-\!\!\!\!| \text{ Factorising}$$

$$\frac{\delta y}{\delta x} = \frac{\cancel{\delta x}[2x + \delta x]}{\cancel{\delta x}} = 2x + \delta x \qquad \textbf{[Equation 2]}$$

If you look at Figure 1.4, as point P_2 moves closer and closer to point P_1, the value of δx gets smaller and smaller, approaching zero. You say that δx tends to zero, or $\delta x \to 0$. Therefore, the gradient of the line P_1P_2 approaches the gradient of the tangent. This can be expressed as follows:

$$\text{Gradient of tangent} = \lim_{\delta x \to 0} \frac{\delta y}{\delta x} = \lim_{\delta x \to 0} (2x + \delta x) = 2x$$

where 'lim' stands for 'limit' and you can say that as δx tends to zero, $2x + \delta x$ approaches $2x$.

You can take the gradient of P_1P_2 as an approximation to the gradient of the tangent at P_1, and consequently you have the rate of change of y with respect to x at the point P_1. The expression $\lim\limits_{\delta x \to 0} \dfrac{\delta y}{\delta x}$ can be applied to other curves, and in calculus, it is denoted by $\dfrac{dy}{dx}$ (read as 'the derivative of y with respect to x'). It is known as the **gradient function** of the curve, or the **derivative** of the function $f(x)$.

Now, if you look at Figure 1.4, the point P_1 is $(x, f(x))$ and point P_2 is $(x + \delta x, f(x + \delta x))$. Therefore, taking the change in y divided by the change in x, you have

$$\frac{\delta y}{\delta x} = \frac{f(x + \delta x) - f(x)}{(x + \delta x) - (x)} = \frac{f(x + \delta x) - f(x)}{\delta x}$$

So, the derivative of the function $f(x)$ is

$$\frac{dy}{dx} = \lim_{\delta x \to 0} \frac{\delta y}{\delta x}$$

$$\frac{dy}{dx} = \lim_{\delta x \to 0} \frac{f(x + \delta x) - f(x)}{\delta x}$$

The process of finding $\dfrac{dy}{dx}$, also denoted by $f'(x)$, is called **differentiation** of the function $y = f(x)$ with respect to x. In other words, when you differentiate $y = f(x)$ with respect to x, you are determining the gradient of the function at any point on the curve or at a specific point on the curve. This can be done based on the concept

$$f'(x) = \lim_{h \to 0} \frac{f(x + h) - f(x)}{h}$$

where δx has been replaced by h. This method of finding the gradient of a function at any point on the curve is called **differentiation from first principles.**

EXAMPLE 1

Differentiate from first principles:

(a) $f(x) = x^2 - 2x$

(b) $f(x) = \dfrac{1}{x^2}$

(c) $f(x) = \sqrt{x}$

(d) $f(x) = (x - 3)^2$

Solution:

(a) $f(x) = x^2 - 2x$

Let h be a small increment in x. Then,

$f(x + h) = (x + h)^2 - 2(x + h)$
$\qquad\quad = x^2 + 2xh + h^2 - 2x - 2h$

$$f'(x) = \lim_{h \to 0} \frac{f(x + h) - f(x)}{h}$$

$$= \lim_{h \to 0} \frac{(x^2 + 2xh + h^2 - 2x - 2h) - (x^2 - 2x)}{h}$$

$$= \lim_{h \to 0} \frac{x^2 + 2xh + h^2 - 2x - 2h - x^2 + 2x}{h}$$

$$= \lim_{h \to 0} \frac{2xh + h^2 - 2h}{h}$$

$$= \lim_{h \to 0} \frac{h(2x + h - 2)}{h}$$

$$= \lim_{h \to 0} (2x + h - 2)$$

$$= (2x - 2) \text{ when } h \to 0$$

$$= \mathbf{(2x - 2)}$$

(b) $f(x) = \dfrac{1}{x^2}$

$$f(x + h) = \frac{1}{(x + h)^2}$$

$$f'(x) = \lim_{h \to 0} \frac{f(x + h) - f(x)}{h}$$

$$= \lim_{h \to 0} \frac{\dfrac{1}{(x + h)^2} - \dfrac{1}{x^2}}{h}$$

$$= \lim_{h \to 0} \frac{\dfrac{x^2 - (x + h)^2}{x^2 \cdot (x + h)^2}}{h}$$

$$= \lim_{h \to 0} \frac{x^2 - (x^2 + 2xh + h^2)}{h \cdot x^2 \cdot (x + h)^2}$$

$$= \lim_{h \to 0} \frac{-2xh - h^2}{h \cdot x^2 \cdot (x + h)^2}$$

$$= \lim_{h \to 0} \frac{h(-2x - h)}{h \cdot x^2 \cdot (x + h)^2}$$

$$= \lim_{h \to 0} \frac{(-2x - h)}{x^2 \cdot (x + h)^2}$$

$$= \frac{-2x}{x^4} \quad \text{when } h \to 0$$

$$= \frac{-2}{x^3}$$

(c) $f(x) = \sqrt{x}$

$f(x + h) = \sqrt{x + h}$

$$f'(x) = \lim_{h \to 0} \frac{f(x + h) - f(x)}{h}$$

$$= \lim_{h \to 0} \frac{\sqrt{x + h} - \sqrt{x}}{h}$$

$$= \lim_{h \to 0} \left[\frac{\sqrt{x+h} - \sqrt{x}}{h} \times \frac{\sqrt{x+h} + \sqrt{x}}{(\sqrt{x+h} + \sqrt{x})} \right]$$

$$= \lim_{h \to 0} \frac{x+h-x}{h \cdot (\sqrt{x+h} + \sqrt{x})}$$

Rationalising the numerator

$$= \lim_{h \to 0} \frac{h}{h \cdot (\sqrt{x+h} + \sqrt{x})}$$

$$= \lim_{h \to 0} \frac{1}{(\sqrt{x+h} + \sqrt{x})}$$

$$= \frac{1}{\sqrt{x} + \sqrt{x}} \quad \text{when } h \to 0$$

$$= \frac{1}{2\sqrt{x}}$$

(d) $f(x) = (x-3)^2$

$f(x+h) = (x+h-3)^2$

$$f'(x) = \lim_{h \to 0} \frac{f(x+h) - f(x)}{h}$$

$$= \lim_{h \to 0} \frac{(x+h-3)^2 - (x-3)^2}{h}$$

$$= \lim_{h \to 0} \frac{(x^2 + xh - 3x + xh + h^2 - 3h - 3x - 3h + 9) - (x^2 - 3x - 3x + 9)}{h}$$

$$= \lim_{h \to 0} \frac{h^2 + 2xh - 6h}{h}$$

$$= \lim_{h \to 0} \frac{h(h + 2x - 6)}{h}$$

$$= \lim_{h \to 0} (h + 2x - 6)$$

$$= 2x - 6 \quad \text{when } h \to 0$$

$$= \mathbf{2x - 6}$$

EXAMPLE 2

Given that $f(x) = \dfrac{1}{\sqrt{x}}$, find $f'(x)$ from first principles.

Solution:

$$f(x) = \frac{1}{\sqrt{x}}$$

Let h be a small increment in the value of x. Then,

$$f(x + h) = \frac{1}{\sqrt{x + h}}$$

$$\frac{f(x + h) - f(x)}{h} = \frac{\dfrac{1}{\sqrt{x + h}} - \dfrac{1}{\sqrt{x}}}{h}$$

$$= \frac{1}{h}\left(\frac{\sqrt{x} - \sqrt{x + h}}{\sqrt{x + h} \cdot \sqrt{x}}\right) \qquad \text{Rationalising the numerator}$$

$$= \frac{1}{h}\left(\frac{\sqrt{x} - \sqrt{x + h}}{\sqrt{x + h} \cdot \sqrt{x}}\right)\left(\frac{\sqrt{x} + \sqrt{x + h}}{\sqrt{x} + \sqrt{x + h}}\right)$$

$$= \frac{1}{h}\left(\frac{x - (x + h)}{x\sqrt{x + h} + (x + h)\sqrt{x}}\right)$$

$$= \frac{1}{h}\left(\frac{-h}{x\sqrt{x + h} + (x + h)\sqrt{x}}\right)$$

$$= \frac{-1}{x\sqrt{x + h} + (x + h)\sqrt{x}}$$

$$f'(x) = \lim_{h \to 0} \frac{f(x + h) - f(x)}{h}$$

$$= \lim_{h \to 0} \frac{-1}{x\sqrt{x + h} + (x + h)\sqrt{x}}$$

$$= \frac{-1}{x\sqrt{x} + x\sqrt{x}} \quad \text{when } h \to 0$$

$$= -\frac{1}{2x\sqrt{x}}$$

$$= -\frac{1}{2x^{\frac{3}{2}}}$$

Fortunately, you do not have to go through this tedious affair of differentiating from first principles all the time. There are some useful formulas and rules which can be utilised to simplify and hasten the process of differentiation. These are explained in the following sections.

THE POWER RULE

The Power Rule enables you to find the derivatives of functions involving powers such as x^5, $\dfrac{1}{x^3}$, $(4x)^{\frac{1}{2}}$ and so on. If $f(x) = x^n$ (where $n \in \mathbb{R}$),

$$\boxed{f'(x) = nx^{n-1}}$$ **[Result (1)]**

EXAMPLE 3

Find the derivative of $2x^3 - 4x^2 + \dfrac{\pi}{2}$ with respect to x.

Solution:

Let $y = 2x^3 - 4x^2 + \dfrac{\pi}{2}$

Then, the derivative is given by

$\dfrac{dy}{dx} = 6x^2 - 8x + 0$ ●—————— $\dfrac{\pi}{2}$ is a constant, and differentiating a constant gives zero

$\quad\ = 6x^2 - 8x$

NOTE

The Sum and Difference Rule: To differentiate a function consisting of a sum (or difference) of several terms, as in Example 3, you find the derivative of each term, then add (or subtract) the derivatives.

If $y = f(x) \pm g(x)$, then $\dfrac{dy}{dx} = f'(x) \pm g'(x)$.

EXAMPLE 4

If $f(x) = \sqrt{x} + \sqrt{2x} + x^e$ (where $e = 2.718$), find $f'(x)$.

Solution:

$$f(x) = \sqrt{x} + \sqrt{2}\sqrt{x} + x^e = x^{\frac{1}{2}} + \sqrt{2}x^{\frac{1}{2}} + x^e$$

$$f'(x) = \frac{1}{2}x^{-\frac{1}{2}} + \sqrt{2} \cdot \frac{1}{2}x^{-\frac{1}{2}} + ex^{e-1} \bullet\!\!-\!\!-\!\!-\!\!| \quad \text{e is the constant 2.718}$$

$$= \frac{1}{2\sqrt{x}} + \frac{\sqrt{2}}{2\sqrt{x}} + ex^{e-1}$$

$$= \frac{1 + \sqrt{2}}{2\sqrt{x}} + ex^{e-1}$$

EXAMPLE 5

Differentiate the following with respect to x.

(a) $\dfrac{5x^4 + 3x^3 - x^2 + 2x}{\sqrt{x}}$

(b) $\dfrac{(3 - 4x)^2}{x^{\frac{3}{2}}}$

Solution:

(a) Let $y = \dfrac{5x^4 + 3x^3 - x^2 + 2x}{\sqrt{x}}$

$$= \dfrac{5x^4 + 3x^3 - x^2 + 2x}{x^{\frac{1}{2}}}$$

$$= \dfrac{5x^4}{x^{\frac{1}{2}}} + \dfrac{3x^3}{x^{\frac{1}{2}}} - \dfrac{x^2}{x^{\frac{1}{2}}} + \dfrac{2x}{x^{\frac{1}{2}}}$$

> **RULES FOR EXPONENTS**
>
> 1. $\dfrac{1}{x^a} = x^{-a}$
> 2. $x^a \cdot x^b = x^{a+b}$ (Multiplication)
> 3. $\dfrac{x^a}{x^b} = x^{a-b}$ (Division)
>
> where a and b are constants.

$$= 5x^{\frac{7}{2}} + 3x^{\frac{5}{2}} - x^{\frac{3}{2}} + 2x^{\frac{1}{2}}$$

Therefore, $\dfrac{dy}{dx} = \dfrac{35}{2}x^{\frac{5}{2}} + \dfrac{15}{2}x^{\frac{3}{2}} - \dfrac{3}{2}x^{\frac{1}{2}} + x^{-\frac{1}{2}}$

$$= \dfrac{35}{2}x^{\frac{5}{2}} + \dfrac{15}{2}x^{\frac{3}{2}} - \dfrac{3}{2}\sqrt{x} + \dfrac{1}{\sqrt{x}}$$

(b) Let $y = \dfrac{(3 - 4x)^2}{x^{\frac{3}{2}}}$

$$= \dfrac{9 - 24x + 16x^2}{x^{\frac{3}{2}}}$$

$$= \dfrac{9}{x^{\frac{3}{2}}} - \dfrac{24x}{x^{\frac{3}{2}}} + \dfrac{16x^2}{x^{\frac{3}{2}}}$$

$$= 9x^{-\frac{3}{2}} - 24x^{-\frac{1}{2}} + 16x^{\frac{1}{2}}$$

Therefore, $\dfrac{dy}{dx} = -\dfrac{27}{2}x^{-\frac{5}{2}} + 12x^{-\frac{3}{2}} + 8x^{-\frac{1}{2}}$

$$= \dfrac{8}{\sqrt{x}} + \dfrac{12}{\sqrt{x^3}} - \dfrac{27}{2\sqrt{x^5}}$$

THE PRODUCT RULE

This rule is used when you have to differentiate a function consisting of the product of two (or more) functions as explained below.

Suppose you have the function $f(x) = uv$ where both u and v are functions of x. The Product Rule states that if $y = uv$ where $u = f_1(x)$ and $v = f_2(x)$, then

$$\boxed{\dfrac{dy}{dx} = u\dfrac{dv}{dx} + v\dfrac{du}{dx}}$$ **[Result (2)]**

The next two examples will illustrate the application of the Product Rule.

EXAMPLE 6

If $f(x) = (x^2 + 2x - 1)(\sqrt{x} + 2)$, find $f'(x)$.

Solution:

Let $u = x^2 + 2x - 1$ and $v = \sqrt{x} + 2$

$$\frac{du}{dx} = 2x + 2 \qquad\qquad\qquad \frac{dv}{dx} = \frac{1}{2}x^{-\frac{1}{2}} = \frac{1}{2\sqrt{x}}$$

Using the Product Rule,

$$\frac{dy}{dx} = u\frac{dv}{dx} + v\frac{du}{dx}$$

$$= (x^2 + 2x - 1)\left(\frac{1}{2\sqrt{x}}\right) + (\sqrt{x} + 2)(2x + 2)$$

$$= \frac{x^2}{2\sqrt{x}} + \frac{2x}{2\sqrt{x}} - \frac{1}{2\sqrt{x}} + 2x^{\frac{3}{2}} + 2\sqrt{x} + 4x + 4$$

$$= \frac{1}{2}x^{\frac{3}{2}} + \sqrt{x} - \frac{1}{2\sqrt{x}} + 2x^{\frac{3}{2}} + 2\sqrt{x} + 4x + 4$$

$$= \frac{5}{2}x^{\frac{3}{2}} + 3\sqrt{x} - \frac{1}{2\sqrt{x}} + 4x + 4$$

Therefore, $f'(x) = \dfrac{5}{2}x^{\frac{3}{2}} + 3\sqrt{x} - \dfrac{1}{2\sqrt{x}} + 4x + 4$

EXAMPLE 7

Differentiate $y = (2\pi x^2 - 7x + 1)(x^2 + 5)$ with respect to x.

Solution:

Let $u = 2\pi x^2 - 7x + 1$ and $v = x^2 + 5$

$$\frac{du}{dx} = 4\pi x - 7 \qquad\qquad \frac{dv}{dx} = 2x$$

Using the Product Rule,

$$\frac{dy}{dx} = u\frac{dv}{dx} + v\frac{du}{dx}$$

$$= (2\pi x^2 - 7x + 1)(2x) + (x^2 + 5)(4\pi x - 7)$$

$$= 4\pi x^3 - 14x^2 + 2x + 4\pi x^3 - 7x^2 + 20\pi x - 35$$

$$= 8\pi x^3 - 21x^2 + (2 + 20\pi)x - 35$$

$$= \mathbf{8\pi x^3 - 21x^2 + 2(1 + 10\pi)x - 35}$$

THE CHAIN RULE

This is one of the most important rules in differentiation and it is encountered in almost all aspects of Calculus, Science and Engineering. It is meant for differentiating composite functions. The notation used for composite functions is a small circle, as in

$g \circ h(x)$. The composite function $g \circ h(x)$ can also be written as $g(h(x))$ which implies that one function lies inside another function.

Consider the function $f(x) = \sqrt{2x - 3}$. You can think of this function as a combination of two functions. If $h(x) = 2x - 3$ and $g(x) = \sqrt{x}$, then the result of substituting $h(x)$ into the function g is

$$g(h(x)) = \sqrt{h(x)} = \sqrt{2x - 3}$$

Differentiation of the composite function $g(h(x))$ can be performed easily by using the **Chain Rule**:

$$\frac{d}{dx}[g(h(x))] = g'(h(x))h'(x)$$

If you have $g \circ h(x)$, then the derivative of the composite function is determined as follows:

$$h(x) = 2x - 3 \quad \text{and} \quad g(2x - 3) = \sqrt{x}$$

$$h'(x) = 2 \qquad\qquad g'(2x - 3) = \frac{1}{2}x^{-\frac{1}{2}} = \frac{1}{2\sqrt{x}}$$

$$\frac{d}{dx}[g \circ h(x)] = \frac{d}{dx}[g(h(x))]$$

$$= g'(h(x))h'(x)$$

$$= \frac{1}{2\sqrt{2x - 3}} \cdot 2 = \frac{1}{\sqrt{2x - 3}}$$

However, if the composite function is $h \circ g(x)$, you will have

$$\frac{d}{dx}[h \circ g(x)] = h'(g(x))g'(x)$$

$$= 2 \cdot \frac{1}{2\sqrt{x}}$$

$$= \frac{1}{\sqrt{x}} \quad \bullet \underline{\hspace{2cm}} \left| \begin{array}{l} \text{This proves that} \\ g \circ h(x) \neq h \circ g(x) \end{array} \right.$$

Based on the explanation above, the Chain Rule can be written as

$$\boxed{\frac{dy}{dx} = \frac{dy}{du} \cdot \frac{du}{dx}} \qquad \textbf{[Result (3)]}$$

given that $y = u(x)$. For example, you can use the Chain Rule to differentiate functions such as $y = (2x + 3)^8$ by taking $y = u^8$ and $u = 2x + 3$. Or you can differentiate $\dfrac{1}{(3x^2 - 2)^{10}}$ by taking $y = \dfrac{1}{u^{10}}$ and $u = 3x^2 - 2$. The following example will illustrate the use of the Chain Rule.

EXAMPLE 8

If $f(x) = \sqrt{1 - 2x^2}$, find $f'(x)$ using the Chain Rule.

Solution:

$$y = \sqrt{1 - 2x^2} = (1 - 2x^2)^{\frac{1}{2}}$$

Let $u = 1 - 2x^2$ and $y = u^{\frac{1}{2}}$

$$\frac{du}{dx} = -4x \qquad \frac{dy}{du} = \frac{1}{2}u^{-\frac{1}{2}} = \frac{1}{2\sqrt{u}}$$

Using the Chain Rule,

$$\frac{dy}{dx} = \frac{dy}{du} \cdot \frac{du}{dx}$$

$$= \frac{1}{2\sqrt{u}} \cdot -4x$$

$$= -\frac{2x}{\sqrt{u}} = -\frac{2x}{\sqrt{1 - 2x^2}}$$

Once you become familiar with this method of differentiation, you will be able to write down the derivative in one simple step as follows:

$$y = (1 - 2x^2)^8$$

$$\frac{dy}{dx} = 8 \cdot (1 - 2x^2)^7 \cdot \frac{d}{dx}(1 - 2x^2) \bullet$$ — The last step being the differentiation of the term inside the parentheses

$$= 8 \cdot (1 - 2x^2)^7 \cdot -4x$$

$$= -32x(1 - 2x^2)^7$$

NOTE

The Power Rule can be derived from the Chain Rule.

In the next example, you will use both the Product Rule and the Chain Rule to determine the derivative.

EXAMPLE 9

If $y = (5x^3 - 2x^2 + 4)\sqrt{1 - x^2}$, find $\dfrac{dy}{dx}$.

Solution:

Let $u = 5x^3 - 2x^2 + 4$ and $v = \sqrt{1 - x^2} = (1 - x^2)^{\frac{1}{2}}$

$$\frac{du}{dx} = 15x^2 - 4x \qquad\qquad \frac{dv}{dx} = \frac{1}{2}(1 - x^2)^{-\frac{1}{2}} \cdot -2x$$

Using the Chain Rule

$$= -\frac{x}{\sqrt{1 - x^2}}$$

Using the Product Rule,

$$\frac{dy}{dx} = u\frac{dv}{dx} + v\frac{du}{dx}$$

$$= (5x^3 - 2x^2 + 4)\left(-\frac{x}{\sqrt{1 - x^2}}\right) + \left(\sqrt{1 - x^2}\right)(15x^2 - 4x)$$

$$= -\frac{5x^4 - 2x^3 + 4x}{\sqrt{1 - x^2}} + (15x^2 - 4x)\left(\sqrt{1 - x^2}\right)$$

$$= \frac{-5x^4 + 2x^3 - 4x + (15x^2 - 4x)(1 - x^2)}{\sqrt{1 - x^2}}$$

$$= \frac{-5x^4 + 2x^3 - 4x + 15x^2 - 15x^4 - 4x + 4x^3}{\sqrt{1 - x^2}}$$

$$= \frac{-20x^4 + 6x^3 + 15x^2 - 8x}{\sqrt{1 - x^2}}$$

THE QUOTIENT RULE

When you need to differentiate a function consisting of two functions, one divided by the other such as $y = \dfrac{u(x)}{v(x)}$, you can use the Quotient Rule as follows:

Given that $y = \dfrac{u(x)}{v(x)}$, then

$$\boxed{\frac{dy}{dx} = \frac{v\dfrac{du}{dx} - u\dfrac{dv}{dx}}{v^2}} \qquad \textbf{[Result (4)]}$$

EXAMPLE 10

Differentiate $y = \dfrac{4 - \sqrt{x}}{4 + \sqrt{x}}$ with respect to x.

Solution:

Let $u = 4 - \sqrt{x} = 4 - (x)^{\frac{1}{2}}$ and $v = 4 + \sqrt{x} = 4 + (x)^{\frac{1}{2}}$

$$\frac{du}{dx} = -\frac{1}{2}(x)^{-\frac{1}{2}}$$

$$\frac{dv}{dx} = \frac{1}{2}(x)^{-\frac{1}{2}}$$

$$= -\frac{1}{2\sqrt{x}}$$

$$= \frac{1}{2\sqrt{x}}$$

Therefore, $\dfrac{dy}{dx} = \dfrac{v\dfrac{du}{dx} - u\dfrac{dv}{dx}}{v^2}$

$$= \frac{\left(4 + \sqrt{x}\right)\left(-\dfrac{1}{2\sqrt{x}}\right) - \left(4 - \sqrt{x}\right)\left(\dfrac{1}{2\sqrt{x}}\right)}{\left(4 + \sqrt{x}\right)^2}$$

$$= \frac{-\dfrac{2}{\sqrt{x}} - \dfrac{1}{2} - \dfrac{2}{\sqrt{x}} + \dfrac{1}{2}}{\left(4 + \sqrt{x}\right)^2}$$

$$= \frac{-\dfrac{4}{\sqrt{x}}}{\left(4 + \sqrt{x}\right)^2}$$

$$= -\frac{4}{\sqrt{x}\left(4 + \sqrt{x}\right)^2}$$

EXAMPLE 11

If $f(x) = \dfrac{1}{5 - 3x}$, find $f'(x)$.

Solution:

You can resolve this by using either the Chain Rule or the Quotient Rule.

Using the Chain Rule:

$$f(x) = \frac{1}{5 - 3x} = (5 - 3x)^{-1}$$

Using the Chain Rule, you obtain

$$f'(x) = -1(5 - 3x)^{-2} \cdot (-3)$$
$$= \frac{3}{(5 - 3x)^2}$$

OR

Using the Quotient Rule:

$$y = \frac{1}{5 - 3x}$$

Let $u = 1$ and $v = 5 - 3x$

$$\frac{du}{dx} = 0 \qquad \frac{dv}{dx} = -3$$

Using the Quotient Rule, you have

$$\frac{dy}{dx} = \frac{v\dfrac{du}{dx} - u\dfrac{dv}{dx}}{v^2}$$

$$= \frac{(5 - 3x)(0) - (1)(-3)}{(5 - 3x)^2}$$

$$= \frac{3}{(5 - 3x)^2}$$

The choice of using either the Quotient Rule or the Chain Rule is left solely to your discretion. Either method is acceptable.

REVIEW QUESTIONS

1. Differentiate the following with respect to x from first principles:

(a) $3x - 5$ (b) $\dfrac{4}{3x}$ (c) $(x + 2)^2$

(d) $\dfrac{1}{x + 4}$ (e) $\sqrt{2x}$ (f) $\dfrac{1}{\sqrt{x + 4}}$

(g) $\dfrac{3x - 2}{5}$ (h) $x^2 - 5x$

2. Find the derivatives of the following functions with respect to x:

(a) $2x^3 - 3x^2 + 4x$

(b) $4x^2 - \dfrac{3}{x^3}$

(c) $3\sqrt{x} - 4x^2$

(d) $4\pi x - \dfrac{3}{\sqrt{x}}$

(e) $\dfrac{4x^2 - 2x + 3}{x}$

(f) $\dfrac{2x^3 - 4x^2 + 3\pi}{\sqrt{x}}$

3. Find $f'(x)$ for each of the following functions:

(a) $f(x) = 4(2x - 3)^7$

(b) $f(x) = \dfrac{3}{(2x + 4)^5}$

(c) $f(x) = (2x^3 - 3x + 2)^3$

(d) $f(x) = \dfrac{2x + 3}{(x + 5)^4}$

(e) $f(x) = (-3x)(x + 3)^5$

(f) $f(x) = \dfrac{3}{(2x^2 - 4x + 5)^3}$

4. Find $\dfrac{dy}{dx}$ of the following functions:

(a) $y = (4x - 3)(x^2 - 4)^3$

(b) $y = \sqrt{x + 3}\,(4\pi x + 5)$

(c) $y = (4x - 5)(x^3 - 2x^2 + 3)$

(d) $y = (\sqrt{x} + 4)(\sqrt{2x} - 3)$

(e) $y = \dfrac{3x - 2}{4x + 3}$

(f) $y = \dfrac{2x + 5}{(4x^2 + 3)^2}$

(g) $y = \dfrac{\sqrt{x + 4}}{(x^2 - 3)^{\frac{3}{2}}}$

(h) $y = \dfrac{2x^3 - 4x}{x^3 - 2x + 4}$

(i) $y = \dfrac{4\pi + \sqrt{x}}{\sqrt{3x - 5}}$

CHAPTER 2

DIFFERENTIATION OF TRIGONOMETRIC FUNCTIONS

INTRODUCTION

When it comes to derivatives, trigonometric functions are one of the least favourite functions among students. However, once students are able to come to grips with the concept, they will soon realise that it is far simpler than it seems. As a matter of fact, trigonometric functions are very useful in the real world, in fields such as astronomy, navigation, physics, engineering, surveying, carpentry and many others. Therefore, knowing how to deal with trigonometric functions will stand students in good stead for the future.

There are six common trigonometric functions, namely, $\sin(x)$, $\cos(x)$, $\tan(x)$, $\cot(x)$, $\sec(x)$ and $\csc(x)$. Basically, they are used to relate the lengths of the sides of a triangle with the angles of the triangle. So, what do the derivatives of these trigonometric functions look like?

It all comes back to the method of differentiation from first principles. Let us consider the function $y = \sin x$. Then, the derivative is given by

$$\frac{dy}{dx} = \lim_{h \to 0} \frac{\sin(x + h) - \sin(x)}{h}$$

$$= \lim_{h \to 0} \frac{\sin(x)\cos(h) + \cos(x)\sin(h) - \sin(x)}{h}$$

Apply the appropriate Sum-Difference formula for sine

$$= \lim_{h \to 0} \frac{\sin(x)\cos(h) - \sin(x) + \cos(x)\sin(h)}{h}$$

Move the term sin(x)

$$= \lim_{h \to 0} \frac{\sin(x)\cos((h) - 1) + \cos(x)\sin(h)}{h}$$

Extract the common factor, sin(x)

$$= \lim_{h \to 0} \frac{\sin(x)(\cos(h) - 1)}{h} + \lim_{h \to 0} \frac{\cos(x)\sin(h)}{h}$$

Separate the limits

$$= \sin(x) \lim_{h \to 0} \frac{(\cos(h) - 1)}{h} + \cos(x) \lim_{h \to 0} \frac{\sin(h)}{h}$$

You are only concerned with the limit of each term as $h \to 0$

NOTE

Sum-Difference Formulas: These formulas involve the sum and difference of two angles, and can be helpful in rearranging expressions in order to solve complex trigonometric equations.

$$\sin(a \pm b) = \sin a \cos b \pm \cos a \sin b$$
$$\cos(a \pm b) = \cos a \cos b \mp \sin a \sin b$$

So, what are the values of $\lim\limits_{h \to 0} \dfrac{(\cos(h) - 1)}{h}$ and $\lim\limits_{h \to 0} \dfrac{\sin(h)}{h}$? For the answer, you can look at the graphs of the respective functions in Figure 2.1 and Figure 2.2.

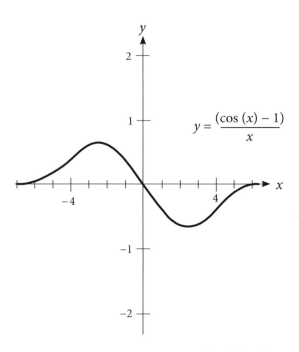

Figure 2.1   Graph of $y = \dfrac{(\cos(x) - 1)}{x}$

Notice that the graph of $y = \dfrac{(\cos(x) - 1)}{x}$ approaches 0 as x approaches 0.

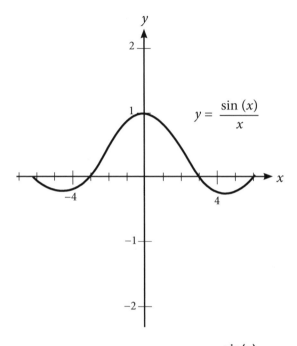

Figure 2.2   Graph of $y = \dfrac{\sin(x)}{x}$

As you can see, the graph of $y = \dfrac{\sin(x)}{x}$ approaches 1 as x approaches 0. The observations from the two graphs imply that

$$\lim_{h \to 0} \frac{(\cos(h) - 1)}{h} = 0 \quad \text{and} \quad \lim_{h \to 0} \frac{\sin(h)}{h} = 1$$

Therefore, $\dfrac{dy}{dx} = \sin(x) \lim\limits_{h \to 0} \dfrac{(\cos(h) - 1)}{h} + \cos(x) \lim\limits_{h \to 0} \dfrac{\sin(h)}{h}$

$$= \sin(x) \cdot 0 + \cos(x) \cdot 1$$

$$= \cos(x)$$

Now, you can try finding the derivative of $y = \cos(x)$ in a similar way by differentiating from first principles. The proof is provided in the Appendix on page 121.

DERIVATIVES OF BASIC TRIGONOMETRIC FUNCTIONS

Here are the derivatives of the six basic trigonometric functions.

1. $\dfrac{d}{dx}(\sin x) = \cos x$

2. $\dfrac{d}{dx}(\cos x) = -\sin x$

3. $\dfrac{d}{dx}(\tan x) = \dfrac{d}{dx}\left(\dfrac{\sin x}{\cos x}\right)$

$\qquad = \dfrac{\cos x(\cos x) - \sin x(-\sin x)}{\cos^2 x}$ ⟵ Using the Quotient Rule

$\qquad = \dfrac{\cos^2 x + \sin^2 x}{\cos^2 x}$

$\qquad = \dfrac{1}{\cos^2 x}$ ⟵ Since $\cos^2 x + \sin^2 x = 1$

$\qquad = \sec^2 x$

4. $\dfrac{d}{dx}(\cot x) = \dfrac{d}{dx}\left(\dfrac{\cos x}{\sin x}\right)$

$\qquad = \dfrac{\sin x(-\sin x) - \cos x(\cos x)}{\sin^2 x}$ • ——| Using the Quotient Rule

$\qquad = \dfrac{-\sin^2 x - \cos^2 x}{\sin^2 x}$

$\qquad = \dfrac{-(\sin^2 x + \cos^2 x)}{\sin^2 x}$

$\qquad = -\dfrac{1}{\sin^2 x} = -\textbf{cosec}^2\ \textbf{x}$

5. $\dfrac{d}{dx}(\sec x) = \dfrac{d}{dx}\left(\dfrac{1}{\cos x}\right) = \dfrac{d}{dx}(\cos x)^{-1}$

$\qquad = -1(\cos x)^{-2} \cdot (-\sin x)$ • ———————| Using the Chain Rule

$\qquad = \dfrac{\sin x}{\cos x \cdot \cos x}$

$\qquad = \dfrac{\sin x}{\cos x} \cdot \dfrac{1}{\cos x}$

$\qquad = \tan x \sec x = \textbf{sec}\ \textbf{x}\ \textbf{tan}\ \textbf{x}$

Alternatively, you can also obtain the same result using the Quotient Rule. You should verify this for yourself.

6. $\dfrac{d}{dx}(\operatorname{cosec} x) = \dfrac{d}{dx}\left(\dfrac{1}{\sin x}\right) = \dfrac{d}{dx}(\sin x)^{-1}$

$= -1(\sin x)^{-2} \cdot (\cos x)$ Using the Chain Rule

$= -\dfrac{\cos x}{\sin x \cdot \sin x}$

$= -\dfrac{\cos x}{\sin^2 x}$

$= -\dfrac{\cos x}{\sin x} \cdot \dfrac{1}{\sin x}$

$= -\cot x \,\operatorname{cosec} x$

OR

$\dfrac{d}{dx}(\operatorname{cosec} x) = \dfrac{d}{dx}\left(\dfrac{1}{\sin x}\right)$

$= \dfrac{\sin x(0) - 1(\cos x)}{\sin^2 x}$

$= -\dfrac{\cos x}{\sin^2 x}$

$= -\dfrac{\cos x}{\sin x} \cdot \dfrac{1}{\sin x}$

$= -\cot x \,\operatorname{cosec} x$

> **TIP**
>
> You will find it easy to remember the derivatives of all the basic trigonometric functions with the aid of the following chart.

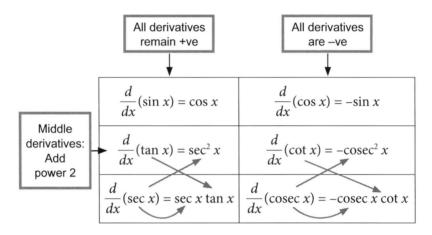

Nevertheless, rather than just committing the above to memory, it is advisable that you first understand how to obtain the derivatives of the trigonometric functions as shown earlier.

EXAMPLE 1

Find $\dfrac{dy}{dx}$ if (a) $y = 2 \sin\left(2x + \dfrac{\pi}{6}\right)$, (b) $y = 3 \cos\left(\pi x + \dfrac{\pi}{3}\right)$

Solution:

Using the Chain Rule,

(a) $y = 2 \sin\left(2x + \dfrac{\pi}{6}\right)$

$\dfrac{dy}{dx} = 2 \cos\left(2x + \dfrac{\pi}{6}\right) \cdot 2$

$= \mathbf{4 \cos\left(2x + \dfrac{\pi}{6}\right)}$

(b) $y = 3 \cos\left(\pi x + \dfrac{\pi}{3}\right)$

$\dfrac{dy}{dx} = 3 \cdot -\sin\left(\pi x + \dfrac{\pi}{3}\right) \cdot \pi$

$= \mathbf{-3\pi \sin\left(\pi x + \dfrac{\pi}{3}\right)}$

EXAMPLE 2

Differentiate with respect to x:

(a) $5 \sin^3(3x)$ (b) $\sin^2(2x)$

(c) $2 \cos(3x^3)$ (d) $3 \cos^4(2x^5)$

Solution:

(a) Let $y = 5 \sin^3(3x)$

$$\frac{dy}{dx} = 5 \cdot 3 \sin^2(3x) \cdot \cos(3x) \cdot 3$$

$$= \mathbf{45 \sin^2(3x) \cos(3x)}$$

(b) Let $y = \sin^2(2x)$

$$\frac{dy}{dx} = 2 \sin(2x) \cdot \cos(2x) \cdot 2$$

$$= \mathbf{4 \sin(2x) \cos(2x)}$$

(c) Let $y = 2 \cos(3x^3)$

$$\frac{dy}{dx} = 2 \cdot -\sin(3x^3) \cdot 9x^2$$

$$= \mathbf{-18x^2 \sin(3x^3)}$$

(d) Let $y = 3 \cos^4(2x^5)$

$$\frac{dy}{dx} = 3(4) \cdot \cos^3(2x^5)$$
$$\cdot -\sin(2x^5) \cdot 10x^4$$

$$= \mathbf{-120x^4 \cos^3(2x^5) \sin(2x^5)}$$

TIP

$\sin^a(x) = (\sin(x))^a$
$\cos^a(x) = (\cos(x))^a$

Let $y = 5u^3$ and
$u = \sin(3x)$, then
apply the Chain Rule.

Let $y = u^2$ and
$u = \sin(2x)$, then
apply the Chain Rule.

Let $y = 2 \cos(u)$ and
$u = 3x^3$, then apply the
Chain Rule.

Let $y = 3 \cos^4(u)$ and
$u = 2x^5$, then apply
the Chain Rule.

Both Example 1 and Example 2 have been solved by using the Chain Rule.

EXAMPLE 3

Differentiate with respect to x:

(a) $\sin^2 x \cos^2 x$ (b) $\sqrt{x} \sin 2x$ (c) $\sin x \tan x$

Solution:

(a) Let $y = \sin^2 x \cos^2 x$

$$\frac{dy}{dx} = u\frac{dv}{dx} + v\frac{du}{dx}$$

$$= \sin^2 x \cdot 2\cos x \cdot (-\sin x) + \cos^2 x \cdot 2\sin x \cdot \cos x$$

$$= -2\cos x \sin^3 x + 2\sin x \cos^3 x$$

$$= 2\sin x \cos x(\cos^2 x - \sin^2 x)$$

$$= \mathbf{\sin 2x \cos 2x} \bullet\!\!\!-\!\!\!-\!\!\!-\!\!\!-\!\!\!-\!\!\!- \quad \text{You are encouraged to verify this for yourself}$$

(b) Let $y = \sqrt{x} \sin 2x$

$$\frac{dy}{dx} = u\frac{dv}{dx} + v\frac{du}{dx}$$

$$= \sqrt{x} \cdot 2\cos 2x + \sin 2x \cdot \frac{1}{2}x^{-\frac{1}{2}}$$

$$= \mathbf{2\sqrt{x}} \cos 2x + \frac{1}{2\sqrt{x}}\sin 2x$$

(c) Let $y = \sin x \tan x$

$$\frac{dy}{dx} = \sin x \sec^2 x + \tan x \cos x \;\; \bullet\!\!-\!\!\mid \begin{array}{l} \text{Applying the} \\ \text{Product Rule} \end{array}$$

$$= \sin x \cdot \left(\frac{1}{\cos^2 x} \right) + \frac{\sin x}{\cos x} \cdot \cos x$$

$$= \frac{\sin x}{\cos x} \cdot \frac{1}{\cos x} + \sin x \cdot \frac{\cos x}{\cos x}$$

$$= \mathbf{\tan x \sec x + \sin x}$$

EXAMPLE 4

Find the derivative of $\pi x \tan (\pi x)$ with respect to x.

Solution:

Let $y = \pi x \tan (\pi x)$

$$\frac{dy}{dx} = \pi x \sec^2 (\pi x) \cdot \pi + \tan (\pi x) \cdot \pi$$

$$= \boldsymbol{\pi^2 x \sec^2 (\pi x) + \pi \tan (\pi x)}$$

EXAMPLE 5

Find the derivative of $\sec x$ and hence, differentiate $\dfrac{\sec^2 x}{\sin x}$ with respect to x.

Solution:

Let $y = \sec x = \dfrac{1}{\cos x}$

$$y = \dfrac{1}{\cos x} = (\cos x)^{-1}$$

$$\dfrac{dy}{dx} = -1(\cos x)^{-2} \cdot (-\sin x) \quad\longleftarrow\quad \text{Using the Chain Rule}$$

$$= \dfrac{\sin x}{\cos^2 x} = \tan x \sec x$$

Therefore, $\dfrac{dy}{dx} = \boldsymbol{\tan x \sec x}$ or $\boldsymbol{\sin x \sec^2 x}$

Let $f(x) = \dfrac{\sec^2 x}{\sin x}$

$$f'(x) = \dfrac{v\dfrac{du}{dx} - u\dfrac{dv}{dx}}{v^2}$$

$$= \dfrac{\sin x \cdot 2\sec x \cdot \tan x \sec x - \sec^2 x \cdot \cos x}{\sin^2 x}$$

$$= \dfrac{2\sin x \dfrac{1}{\cos x} \cdot \dfrac{\sin x}{\cos x} \cdot \dfrac{1}{\cos x} - \dfrac{1}{\cos^2 x}\cos x}{\sin^2 x}$$

$$= \dfrac{\dfrac{2\sin^2 x}{\cos^3 x} - \dfrac{1}{\cos x}}{\sin^2 x}$$

$$= \left[\dfrac{\boldsymbol{2\sin^2 x - \cos^2 x}}{\boldsymbol{\sin^2 x \cos^3 x}}\right]$$

EXAMPLE 6

Differentiate $\dfrac{\pi x^3}{\cos 2\pi x}$ with respect to x.

Solution:

Let $y = \dfrac{\pi x^3}{\cos 2\pi x}$ where $u = \pi x^3$ and $v = \cos 2\pi x$

$$\frac{du}{dx} = 3\pi x^2 \qquad \frac{dv}{dx} = -2\pi \sin 2\pi x$$

$$\frac{dy}{dx} = \frac{v\dfrac{du}{dx} - u\dfrac{dv}{dx}}{v^2}$$

$$= \frac{\cos 2\pi x \cdot 3\pi x^2 - \pi x^3 \cdot (-2\pi \sin 2\pi x)}{\cos^2 2\pi x}$$

$$= \frac{3\pi x^2 \cos 2\pi x + 2\pi^2 x^3 \sin 2\pi x}{\cos^2 2\pi x}$$

EXAMPLE 7

Find the derivative of $y = \tan(\sin^2 x)$ with respect to x.

Solution:

$$y = \tan(\sin^2 x)$$

$$\frac{dy}{dx} = \sec^2(\sin^2 x) \cdot 2\sin x \cos x$$

$$\qquad = \mathbf{2\sin x \cos x \sec^2(\sin^2 x)}$$

EXAMPLE 8

Find $\dfrac{d}{dx}[\sin(\tan x)]$.

Solution:

$$\dfrac{d}{dx}[\sin(\tan x)] = \mathbf{\cos(\tan x) \cdot \sec^2 x}$$

EXAMPLE 9

Find the derivative of $(\tan x + \cos x)^3$ with respect to x.

Solution:

Let $y = (\tan x + \cos x)^3$

$$\dfrac{dy}{dx} = \mathbf{3(\tan x + \cos x)^2 \cdot (\sec^2 x - \sin x)}$$

EXAMPLE 10

Differentiate $\dfrac{\tan x}{\sec x - 1}$ with respect to x.

Solution:

Let $y = \dfrac{\tan x}{\sec x - 1}$

$$\frac{dy}{dx} = \frac{v\,\dfrac{du}{dx} - u\,\dfrac{dv}{dx}}{v^2}$$

$$= \frac{(\sec x - 1) \cdot \sec^2 x - \tan x \cdot \tan x \sec x}{(\sec x - 1)^2}$$

$$= \frac{\sec^3 x - \sec^2 x - \tan^2 x \sec x}{(\sec x - 1)^2}$$

$$= \frac{\sec x(\sec^2 x - \sec x - \tan^2 x)}{(\sec x - 1)^2}$$

Using the identity $\sec^2 x = 1 + \tan^2 x$, and therefore $\tan^2 x = \sec^2 x - 1$, the last equation can be simplified to

$$\frac{dy}{dx} = \frac{\sec x(\sec^2 x - \sec x - (\sec^2 x - 1))}{(\sec x - 1)^2}$$

$$= \frac{\sec x(1 - \sec x)}{(\sec x - 1)^2}$$

$$= \frac{-\sec x(\sec x - 1)}{(\sec x - 1)^2}$$

$$= -\frac{\sec x}{\sec x - 1}$$

EXAMPLE 11

If $f(x) = \dfrac{x}{\sqrt{\sin(2x) - 1}}$, find $f'(x)$.

Solution:

$$f'(x) = \frac{v\dfrac{du}{dx} - u\dfrac{dv}{dx}}{v^2}$$

$$= \frac{\sqrt{\sin(2x) - 1} \cdot 1 - x \cdot \dfrac{1}{2}(\sin(2x) - 1)^{-\frac{1}{2}} \cdot 2\cos(2x)}{\left(\sqrt{\sin(2x) - 1}\right)^2}$$

$$= \frac{\sqrt{\sin(2x) - 1} - \dfrac{x \cdot \cos(2x)}{\sqrt{\sin(2x) - 1}}}{(\sin(2x) - 1)}$$

$$= \frac{\sin(2x) - 1 - x \cdot \cos(2x)}{(\sin(2x) - 1)^{\frac{3}{2}}}$$

REVIEW QUESTIONS

1. Differentiate the following with respect to x:

   (a) $2\pi \sin(4x - 3)$ (b) $5\pi \tan(5 - 2x)$

   (c) $\dfrac{\pi}{5}\cos(3x + 2\pi)$ (d) $2\pi \sec\left(\pi x - \dfrac{3}{\pi}\right)$

   (e) $4\operatorname{cosec}(3x + 2\pi)$ (f) $\dfrac{3}{\pi}\cot\left(\dfrac{\pi}{6} - 2\pi x\right)$

   (g) $3\pi\operatorname{cosec}(3x^2 + 4\pi)$

2. Find $f'(x)$ for the following functions:

(a) $f(x) = 4x \sin(2\pi x)$

(b) $f(x) = \dfrac{2}{x} \cos(3x + 4\pi)$

(c) $f(x) = 5\pi \cot^3(4x)$

(d) $f(x) = 5 \sec^2(4x^3)$

(e) $f(x) = \cos^3 x \tan^2 x$

(f) $f(x) = \sqrt{\pi x}\, \operatorname{cosec}(2\pi x)$

(g) $f(x) = 5\pi x \operatorname{cosec}(2x - 5)$

(h) $f(x) = 2x^{-3} \sec(\pi x^3)$

3. Find $\dfrac{dy}{dx}$ of the following:

(a) $y = \dfrac{\sin^2 x}{\operatorname{cosec} x}$

(b) $y = \dfrac{\cot(2\pi x)}{4\pi x^2}$

(c) $y = \cos^2(\cot x)$

(d) $y = \sin^3 (\sec x)$

(e) $y = \dfrac{\cos x}{\sin x - 1}$

(f) $y = \dfrac{\cot x}{\operatorname{cosec} x - 1}$

(g) $y = (\sin(2x) - \cot(2x))^3$

(h) $y = \dfrac{2x}{\sqrt{\cos(x) + 2}}$

(i) $y = \dfrac{\sqrt{\tan(2x) - 5}}{x^2}$

CHAPTER 3

DERIVATIVES OF EXPONENTIAL AND LOGARITHMIC FUNCTIONS

DERIVATIVES OF EXPONENTIAL FUNCTIONS

Exponential functions are often a source of anxiety among students. This group of functions is much misunderstood. It is the writers' intention to eliminate this irrational fear from the minds of students.

Exponential functions, such as $y = 2^x$, $y = 3^x$ and $y = 2^{-x}$, differ from polynomial and trigonometric functions in that the base of the exponential function is a pure constant, like 2 or 3, while the index is the variable x. When you differentiate such functions, you do so with respect to the index x which is the variable.

Let us try to differentiate $y = 2.718^x$ with a base value between 2 and 3, say 2.718. In Mathematics, this special base of 2.718 is denoted by the special symbol e. In other words, you want to differentiate $y = 2.718^x = e^x$.

This is the only base that will enable you to differentiate exponential functions in two simple steps.

EXAMPLE 1

The exponential function $y = e^x$ is the most fundamental among the exponential functions. Differentiate y with respect to x.

Solution:

To differentiate $y = e^x$, there are only two steps.

$$y = e^x$$

$$\frac{dy}{dx}(e^x) = e^x \cdot \frac{d}{dx}(x) = e^x \cdot 1 = e^x$$

STEP 1: Copy the given function.

STEP 2: Differentiate the index x and multiply the result with the given function.

Therefore, if $y = e^x$,

$$\frac{dy}{dx} = e^x \cdot 1 = e^x$$

EXAMPLE 2

Find the derivative of $y = e^{-x}$ with respect to x.

Solution:

First, copy the given function e^{-x}. Next, differentiate the index $-x$ to give you -1, and multiply that to the expression from the first step:

$$\frac{dy}{dx} = e^{-x} \cdot \frac{d}{dx}(-x)$$

$$= e^{-x} \cdot -1$$

$$= -e^{-x}$$

EXAMPLE 3

Differentiate $y = e^{\pi}$ with respect to x.

Solution:

Before you rush off to differentiate this function, let us pause to consider the given function. It has been mentioned earlier that e is a constant with a value of 2.718. Therefore, the function $y = e^{\pi}$ is a constant raised to the power of another constant π. Overall $y = e^{\pi}$ is just a constant and differentiating any constant will produce zero.

Therefore, $\dfrac{d}{dx}(e^{\pi}) = \mathbf{0}$

EXAMPLE 4

Find the value of the derivative of $y = e^{\pi x}$ at $x = 0$.

Solution:

Remember that π is a constant of value 3.142; this means that you need to differentiate $y = e^{3.142x}$.

Using the two-step procedure,

$$\frac{dy}{dx} = e^{\pi x} \cdot \pi = \pi e^{\pi x}$$

When $x = 0$, $\dfrac{dy}{dx} = \pi e^0 = \pi \cdot 1 = \boldsymbol{\pi}$

EXAMPLE 5

Differentiate $y = e^{\sqrt{x}}$ with respect to x.

Solution:

Using the two-step procedure,

$$\frac{dy}{dx} = e^{\sqrt{x}} \cdot \frac{d}{dx}\left(\sqrt{x}\right)$$

$$= e^{\sqrt{x}} \cdot \frac{1}{2}x^{-\frac{1}{2}} = \frac{1}{2\sqrt{x}} \cdot e^{\sqrt{x}} = \frac{e^{\sqrt{x}}}{2\sqrt{x}}$$

An exponential function interacts freely with other functions while retaining its unique characteristics. This is evident in the next example.

EXAMPLE 6

Find $\dfrac{dy}{dx}$ if $y = e^{\cos^2 x}$.

Solution:

The two-step solution is laid out below.

$$y = e^{\cos^2 x}$$

$$\frac{dy}{dx} = e^{\cos^2 x} \cdot \frac{d}{dx}(\cos^2 x)$$

$$= e^{\cos^2 x} \cdot 2\cos x \cdot (-\sin x)$$

$$= -2\sin x \cos x \cdot e^{\cos^2 x}$$

EXAMPLE 7

Differentiate $f(x) = xe^{x^2}$ with respect to x.

Solution:

This problem requires the application of the Product Rule as follows:

$$y = \underset{u}{x}\underset{v}{e^{x^2}}$$

$$\frac{dy}{dx} = x \cdot \frac{d}{dx}(e^{x^2}) + e^{x^2} \cdot \frac{d}{dx}(x)$$

$$= x \cdot e^{x^2} \cdot 2x + e^{x^2} \cdot 1$$

$$= e^{x^2}(2x^2 + 1)$$

EXAMPLE 8

If $f(x) = e^{\frac{1}{x^2}}$, find $f'(x)$.

Solution:

$$f(x) = e^{\frac{1}{x^2}}$$

$$f'(x) = e^{\frac{1}{x^2}} \cdot -2x^{-3}$$

$$= \frac{-2e^{\frac{1}{x^2}}}{x^3}$$

EXAMPLE 9

If $f(x) = e^{\sec x}$, find $f'(x)$.

Solution:

$$f(x) = e^{\sec x}$$
$$f'(x) = e^{\sec x} \cdot \frac{d}{dx}(\sec x)$$
$$= e^{\sec x} \cdot \frac{d}{dx}(\cos x)^{-1}$$
$$= e^{\sec x} \cdot -1(\cos x)^{-2} \cdot (-\sin x) \quad \longleftarrow \quad \text{Applying the Chain Rule}$$
$$= e^{\sec x} \cdot \frac{\sin x}{\cos x \cos x} = e^{\sec x} \cdot \tan x \sec x$$

EXAMPLE 10

Find $f'(x)$ if $f(x) = e^{\sqrt{2x}}$.

Solution:

$$f(x) = e^{\sqrt{2x}}$$
$$f'(x) = e^{\sqrt{2x}} \cdot \frac{d}{dx}(\sqrt{2x})$$
$$= e^{\sqrt{2x}} \cdot \frac{d}{dx}(2x)^{\frac{1}{2}}$$
$$= e^{\sqrt{2x}} \cdot \frac{1}{2}(2x)^{-\frac{1}{2}} \cdot 2 = \frac{e^{\sqrt{2x}}}{\sqrt{2x}}$$

EXAMPLE 11

Differentiate $y = e^{2-x}$ with respect to x.

Solution:

$$y = e^{2-x}$$

$$\frac{dy}{dx} = e^{2-x} \cdot -1 = -e^{2-x}$$

EXAMPLE 12

Find $f'(x)$ if $f(x) = \cos(e^x) + e^{\sin x \cos x}$.

Solution:

$$f(x) = \cos(e^x) + e^{\sin x \cos x}$$

$$f'(x) = -\sin(e^x) \cdot e^x \cdot 1 + e^{\sin x \cos x} \cdot \frac{d}{dx}(\sin x \cos x)$$

$$= -e^x \sin(e^x) + e^{\sin x \cos x} \cdot [\sin x \cdot (-\sin x) + \cos x \cdot \cos x]$$

$$= -e^x \sin(e^x) + e^{\sin x \cos x} (\cos^2 x - \sin^2 x)$$

$$= -e^x \sin(e^x) + e^{\sin x \cos x} \cos(2x)$$

Since $\cos(2x) = \cos^2 x - \sin^2 x$

EXAMPLE 13

If $y = \dfrac{1}{1 + 10e^{-\frac{1}{2}t}}$, find $\dfrac{dy}{dt}$.

Solution:

$$y = \frac{1}{1 + 10e^{-\frac{1}{2}t}}$$

$$= \left(1 + 10e^{-\frac{1}{2}t}\right)^{-1}$$

$$\frac{dy}{dt} = -\left(1 + 10e^{-\frac{1}{2}t}\right)^{-2} \cdot \frac{d}{dt}\left(1 + 10e^{-\frac{1}{2}t}\right) \qquad \begin{array}{l} \text{Using the} \\ \text{Chain Rule} \end{array}$$

$$= -\frac{1}{\left(1 + 10e^{-\frac{1}{2}t}\right)^{2}} \cdot 10e^{-\frac{1}{2}t} \cdot -\frac{1}{2}$$

$$= \frac{5e^{-\frac{1}{2}t}}{\left(1 + 10e^{-\frac{1}{2}t}\right)^{2}}$$

$$= \frac{5}{e^{\frac{1}{2}t}\left(1 + 10e^{-\frac{1}{2}t}\right)^{2}}$$

EXAMPLE 14

Find the derivative of $g(x) = \sqrt{2x}\, e^{x^2}$ with respect to x.

Solution:

$$g(x) = \sqrt{2x}\, e^{x^2}$$

$$= \underbrace{(2x)^{\frac{1}{2}}}_{u}\underbrace{e^{x^2}}_{v}$$

$$g'(x) = (2x)^{\frac{1}{2}} \cdot \frac{d}{dx}(e^{x^2}) + e^{x^2} \cdot \frac{d}{dx}\left((2x)^{\frac{1}{2}}\right) \quad\longleftarrow\quad \begin{array}{l}\text{Using the}\\ \text{Product Rule}\\ \text{with } u = (2x)^{\frac{1}{2}}\\ \text{and } v = e^{x^2}\end{array}$$

$$= (2x)^{\frac{1}{2}} \cdot e^{x^2} \cdot 2x + e^{x^2} \cdot \frac{1}{2}(2x)^{-\frac{1}{2}} \cdot 2$$

$$= \sqrt{2x} \cdot 2xe^{x^2} + \frac{e^{x^2}}{\sqrt{2x}}$$

$$= 2\sqrt{2}x^{\frac{3}{2}}e^{x^2} + \frac{e^{x^2}}{\sqrt{2x}}$$

EXAMPLE 15

Differentiate $f(x) = e^x \sin \pi x$ with respect to x.

Solution:

$$f(x) = \underbrace{e^x}_{u}\underbrace{\sin \pi x}_{v}$$

$$f'(x) = e^x \cdot \frac{d}{dx}(\sin \pi x) + \sin \pi x \cdot \frac{d}{dx}(e^x)$$

$$= e^x \cdot \pi \cos \pi x + \sin \pi x \cdot e^x \cdot 1$$

$$= e^x(\pi \cos \pi x + \sin \pi x)$$

EXAMPLE 16

Differentiate $y = e^{\pi e^x}$ with respect to x.

Solution:

$$y = e^{\pi e^x}$$

$$\frac{dy}{dx} = e^{\pi e^x} \cdot \frac{d}{dx}(\pi e^x)$$

$$= e^{\pi e^x} \cdot \pi \cdot e^x \cdot 1$$

$$= \pi e^x e^{\pi e^x}$$

$$= \pi \cdot e^{x + \pi e^x}$$

EXAMPLE 17

Find the derivative of $y = \sin\left(\dfrac{e^x + 1}{e^{-x} - 1}\right)$ with respect to x.

Solution:

$$y = \sin\left(\frac{e^x + 1}{e^{-x} - 1}\right)$$

$$\frac{dy}{dx} = \cos\left(\frac{e^x + 1}{e^{-x} - 1}\right) \cdot \frac{d}{dx}\left(\frac{e^x + 1}{e^{-x} - 1}\right)$$

$$= \cos\left(\frac{e^x + 1}{e^{-x} - 1}\right) \cdot \left[\frac{(e^{-x} - 1) \cdot e^x - (e^x + 1) \cdot e^{-x} \cdot -1}{(e^{-x} - 1)^2}\right]$$

$$= \cos\left(\frac{e^x + 1}{e^{-x} - 1}\right)\left[\frac{e^x(e^{-x} - 1) + e^{-x}(e^x + 1)}{(e^{-x} - 1)^2}\right]$$

$$= \cos\left(\frac{e^x + 1}{e^{-x} - 1}\right)\left[\frac{e^x \cdot e^{-x} - e^x + e^{-x} \cdot e^x + e^{-x}}{(e^{-x} - 1)^2}\right]$$

$$= \cos\left(\frac{e^x + 1}{e^{-x} - 1}\right)\left[\frac{e^{x-x} - e^x + e^{-x+x} + e^{-x}}{(e^{-x} - 1)^2}\right]$$

$$= \cos\left(\frac{e^x + 1}{e^{-x} - 1}\right)\left[\frac{e^0 - e^x + e^0 + e^{-x}}{(e^{-x} - 1)^2}\right]$$

$$= \cos\left(\frac{e^x + 1}{e^{-x} - 1}\right)\left[\frac{2 - e^x + e^{-x}}{(e^{-x} - 1)^2}\right]$$

$$= \left[\frac{2 - e^x + e^{-x}}{(e^{-x} - 1)^2}\right]\cos\left(\frac{e^x + 1}{e^{-x} - 1}\right)$$

EXAMPLE 18

Find the derivative of $y = \sqrt{xe^{-x} - 2}$ with respect to x.

Solution:

$$y = \sqrt{xe^{-x} - 2}$$

$$= (xe^{-x} - 2)^{\frac{1}{2}}$$

$$\frac{dy}{dx} = \frac{1}{2}(xe^{-x} - 2)^{-\frac{1}{2}} \cdot \frac{d}{dx}(xe^{-x} - 2)$$

$$= \frac{1}{2\sqrt{xe^{-x} - 2}} \cdot \left(\frac{d}{dx}(xe^{-x}) - \frac{d}{dx}(2)\right)$$

$$= \frac{1}{2\sqrt{xe^{-x} - 2}} \cdot (x \cdot e^{-x} \cdot -1 + e^{-x} \cdot 1 - 0)$$

$$= \frac{1}{2\sqrt{xe^{-x} - 2}} \cdot (-xe^{-x} + e^{-x})$$

$$= \frac{e^{-x}(-x + 1)}{2\sqrt{xe^{-x} - 2}}$$

$$= \frac{e^{-x}(1 - x)}{2\sqrt{xe^{-x} - 2}}$$

DERIVATIVES OF LOGARITHMIC FUNCTIONS

Many students would throw their arms up in despair whenever they encounter problems involving the derivatives of logarithmic functions. Some students would not even attempt to answer the question, preferring to leave the answer column empty. However, the truth is that logarithmic functions are really not too difficult to handle once you understand the fundamental steps.

Let us begin by looking at the logarithmic function $y = \log_e x$ (also written as $y = \ln x$). It is the inverse of the exponential function $y = e^x$ as shown below:

$$y = e^x$$

Interchanging the x-axis and y-axis, you have

$$x = e^y$$
$$y \ln e = \ln x$$
$$\boldsymbol{y = \ln x} \quad \bullet\!\!-\!\!\mid \text{ Since } \ln e = 1$$

Thus, if you have $y = \log_e x$ (or $y = \ln x$), the derivative of the logarithmic function is $\dfrac{dy}{dx} = \dfrac{1}{x}$.

Like exponential functions, differentiating a logarithmic function also involves two steps.

$$y = \log_e x$$

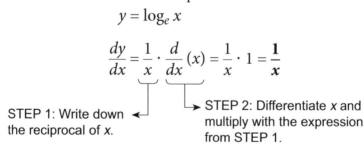

$$\frac{dy}{dx} = \frac{1}{x} \cdot \frac{d}{dx}(x) = \frac{1}{x} \cdot 1 = \frac{1}{x}$$

STEP 1: Write down the reciprocal of x.

STEP 2: Differentiate x and multiply with the expression from STEP 1.

EXAMPLE 19

Differentiate $y = \log_e (6x)$ with respect to x.

Solution:

$$y = \log_e (6x)$$

$$\frac{dy}{dx} = \frac{1}{6x} \cdot \frac{d}{dx}(6x) = \frac{1}{6x} \cdot 6 = \frac{1}{x}$$

Is there another way of differentiating this function? (**Hint:** The answer lies in the laws of logarithm.)

EXAMPLE 20

Find the derivative of each of the following functions with respect to x:

(a) $\ln x \cos^2 x$ (b) $\sqrt{x} \ln(5x)$ (c) $\dfrac{\ln x}{e^x}$

(d) $\sqrt{2x} \log_e \sqrt{2x}$ (e) $\ln(3x - 2)^5$

Solution:

(a) Let $y = \underbrace{\ln x}_{u} \underbrace{\cos^2 x}_{v}$

Applying the Product Rule, you have

$$\frac{dy}{dx} = \ln x \cdot \frac{d}{dx}(\cos^2 x) + \cos^2 x \cdot \frac{d}{dx}(\ln x)$$

$$= \ln x \cdot 2(\cos x) \cdot (-\sin x) + \cos^2 x \cdot \frac{1}{x}$$

$$= -2 \sin x \cos x \ln x + \frac{\cos^2 x}{x}$$

(b) Let $y = \sqrt{x}\,\ln(5x)$

$$\frac{dy}{dx} = \sqrt{x} \cdot \frac{d}{dx}\left(\ln(5x)\right) + \ln(5x) \cdot \frac{d}{dx}\left(\sqrt{x}\right)$$

$$= \sqrt{x} \cdot \frac{1}{5x} \cdot 5 + \ln(5x) \cdot \frac{1}{2}x^{-\frac{1}{2}}$$

$$= \frac{5\sqrt{x}}{5x} + \frac{\ln(5x)}{2\sqrt{x}}$$

$$= \frac{1}{\sqrt{x}} + \frac{\ln(5x)}{2\sqrt{x}}$$

$$= \frac{2 + \ln(5x)}{2\sqrt{x}}$$

(c) Let $y = \dfrac{\ln x}{e^x}$

Instead of using the Quotient Rule to differentiate this function, you can rewrite it as $y = e^{-x}\ln x$. This will let you use the Product Rule instead.

$$\frac{dy}{dx} = e^{-x} \cdot \frac{d}{dx}\left(\ln x\right) + \ln x \cdot \frac{d}{dx}\left(e^{-x}\right)$$

$$= e^{-x} \cdot \frac{1}{x} + \ln x \cdot e^{-x} \cdot -1$$

$$= \frac{1}{xe^x} - \frac{\ln x}{e^x}$$

(d) Let $y = \sqrt{2x} \log_e \sqrt{2x}$

$$\frac{dy}{dx} = \sqrt{2x} \cdot \frac{d}{dx}(\log_e \sqrt{2x}) + \log_e \sqrt{2x} \cdot \frac{d}{dx}(\sqrt{2x})$$

$$= \sqrt{2x} \cdot \frac{1}{\sqrt{2x}} \cdot \frac{1}{2}(2x)^{-\frac{1}{2}} \cdot 2 + \log_e \sqrt{2x} \cdot \frac{1}{2}(2x)^{-\frac{1}{2}} \cdot 2$$

$$= \sqrt{2x} \cdot \frac{1}{\sqrt{2x}} \cdot \frac{2}{2\sqrt{2x}} + \frac{2\log_e \sqrt{2x}}{2\sqrt{2x}}$$

$$= \frac{1}{\sqrt{2x}} + \frac{\log_e \sqrt{2x}}{\sqrt{2x}}$$

$$= \frac{1 + \log_e \sqrt{2x}}{\sqrt{2x}}$$

(e) Let $y = \ln(3x - 2)^5$

This looks complicated, but you can apply the Chain Rule to help you differentiate this function.

Now, let $y = \ln(u)$ and $u = (3x - 2)^5$

$$\frac{dy}{du} = \frac{1}{u} \qquad \frac{du}{dx} = 5(3x - 2)^4 \cdot 3$$

$$= 15(3x - 2)^4$$

 NOTE

$\ln(3x - 2)^5$ is not the same as $(\ln(3x - 2))^5$ or $\ln^5(3x - 2)$.

$$\frac{dy}{dx} = \frac{dy}{du} \cdot \frac{du}{dx} \quad \bullet\!\!-\!\!-\!\!-\!\!-\!\!-\!\!-\!\!-\!\!-\!\!-\!\!| \text{ The Chain Rule}$$

$$\frac{dy}{dx} = \frac{1}{(3x-2)^5} \cdot 15(3x-2)^4 \quad \begin{array}{l} \text{Substitute} \\ u = (3x-2)^5 \end{array}$$

$$= \frac{15}{3x-2} \quad \begin{array}{l} \text{Since } \dfrac{(3x-2)^4}{(3x-2)^5} \\[2mm] = \dfrac{1}{3x-2} \end{array}$$

EXAMPLE 21

Find the derivative of $f(x) = \log_e(\pi x + \tan^2 x)$ with respect to x.

Solution:

$$f(x) = \log_e(\pi x + \tan^2 x)$$

$$f'(x) = \frac{1}{\pi x + \tan^2 x} \cdot \frac{d}{dx}(\pi x + \tan^2 x)$$

$$= \frac{1}{\pi x + \tan^2 x} \cdot (\pi + 2\tan x \sec^2 x)$$

$$= \frac{\pi + 2\tan x \sec^2 x}{\pi x + \tan^2 x}$$

EXAMPLE 22

Find the derivatives of:

(a) $y = \dfrac{\ln x}{\cos x}$

(b) $y = \dfrac{x^2 + 1}{\ln 2x}$

(c) $y = \dfrac{e^x}{e \ln x}$

(d) $y = \dfrac{\log_e(4x - 3)}{\tan x}$

Solution:

You can use the Quotient Rule to differentiate each of the given functions.

(a) $y = \dfrac{\ln x}{\cos x}$

$$\frac{dy}{dx} = \frac{\cos x \cdot \dfrac{d}{dx}(\ln x) - \ln x \cdot \dfrac{d}{dx}(\cos x)}{\cos^2 x}$$

$$= \frac{\cos x \cdot \dfrac{1}{x} - \ln x \cdot (-\sin x)}{\cos^2 x}$$

$$= \frac{\dfrac{\cos x}{x} + \ln x \cdot \sin x}{\cos^2 x}$$

$$= \frac{\cos x + x \ln x \sin x}{x \cos^2 x}$$

(b) $y = \dfrac{x^2 + 1}{\ln 2x}$

$$\frac{dy}{dx} = \frac{\ln 2x \cdot \dfrac{d}{dx}(x^2 + 1) - (x^2 + 1) \cdot \dfrac{d}{dx}(\ln 2x)}{(\ln 2x)^2}$$

$$= \frac{\ln 2x \cdot 2x - (x^2 + 1) \cdot \dfrac{1}{2x} \cdot 2}{(\ln 2x)^2}$$

$$= \frac{2x \ln 2x - \dfrac{x^2 + 1}{x}}{(\ln 2x)^2}$$

$$= \frac{2x^2 \ln 2x - x^2 - 1}{x(\ln 2x)^2}$$

(c) $y = \dfrac{e^x}{e \ln x}$

$$\frac{dy}{dx} = \frac{e \ln x \cdot e^x \cdot 1 - e^x \cdot e \cdot \dfrac{1}{x}}{(e \ln x)^2}$$

$$= \frac{e \cdot e^x \ln x - \dfrac{e \cdot e^x}{x}}{(e \ln x)^2}$$

$$= \frac{e^{1+x} \ln x - \dfrac{e^{1+x}}{x}}{(e \ln x)^2}$$

$$= \frac{xe^{x+1} \ln x - e^{x+1}}{x(e \ln x)^2}$$

$$= \frac{e^{x+1}(x \ln x - 1)}{x(e \ln x)^2}$$

(d) $y = \dfrac{\log_e(4x - 3)}{\tan x}$

$\dfrac{dy}{dx} = \dfrac{\tan x \cdot \dfrac{1}{4x - 3} \cdot 4 - \ln(4x - 3) \cdot \sec^2 x}{\tan^2 x}$

NOTE

$\log_e x = \ln x$

$= \dfrac{\dfrac{4 \tan x}{4x - 3} - \sec^2 x \ln(4x - 3)}{\tan^2 x}$

$= \dfrac{\dfrac{4 \tan x}{4x - 3}}{\tan^2 x} - \dfrac{\sec^2 x \ln(4x - 3)}{\tan^2 x}$

$= \left[\dfrac{4 \tan x}{4x - 3} \div \tan^2 x \right] - \left[\dfrac{1}{\cos^2 x} \ln(4x - 3) \div \dfrac{\sin^2 x}{\cos^2 x} \right]$

$= \left[\dfrac{4 \tan x}{4x - 3} \times \dfrac{1}{\tan^2 x} \right] - \left[\dfrac{1}{\cos^2 x} \ln(4x - 3) \times \dfrac{\cos^2 x}{\sin^2 x} \right]$

When changing from division to multiplication, the numerator and denominator swap positions

$= \left[\dfrac{4}{4x - 3} \times \dfrac{1}{\tan x} \right] - \left[\dfrac{1}{\sin^2 x} \ln(4x - 3) \right]$

$= \dfrac{4 \cot x}{4x - 3} - \ln(4x - 3) \, \text{cosec}^2 x$

EXAMPLE 23

Find the derivative of $y = \log_e((e^x)(e^x - 5))$ with respect to x.

Solution:

To differentiate this using the Product Rule will be difficult. Instead, you can simplify the function by using the law of logarithm involving the product of two functions, that is,

$$\log_e(A \cdot B) = \log_e A + \log_e B$$

Therefore, $y = \log_e((e^x)(e^x - 5))$ can be written as

$$y = \log_e(e^x) + \log_e(e^x - 5)$$

$$\frac{dy}{dx} = \frac{1}{e^x} \cdot \frac{d}{dx}(e^x) + \frac{1}{e^x - 5} \cdot \frac{d}{dx}(e^x - 5)$$

$$= 1 + \frac{e^x}{e^x - 5}$$

$$= \frac{e^x - 5}{e^x - 5} + \frac{e^x}{e^x - 5}$$

$$= \frac{2e^x - 5}{e^x - 5}$$

EXAMPLE 24

Find the derivative of $y = \log_e\left(\dfrac{e^x + e^{-x}}{e^x - e^{-x}}\right)$ with respect to x.

Solution:

Using the law of logarithm involving the quotient of two logarithmic functions, that is,

$$\log_e \left(\frac{A}{B} \right) = \log_e A - \log_e B$$

then, $y = \log_e \left(\dfrac{e^x + e^{-x}}{e^x - e^{-x}} \right)$ can be written as

$$y = \log_e (e^x + e^{-x}) - \log_e (e^x - e^{-x})$$

$$\frac{dy}{dx} = \frac{1}{e^x + e^{-x}} \cdot \frac{d}{dx} (e^x + e^{-x}) - \frac{1}{e^x - e^{-x}} \cdot \frac{d}{dx} (e^x - e^{-x})$$

$$= \frac{e^x - e^{-x}}{e^x + e^{-x}} - \frac{e^x + e^{-x}}{e^x - e^{-x}}$$

REVIEW QUESTIONS

1. Differentiate the following with respect to x:

   (a) $4e^{2x} - \dfrac{3}{e^{x^2}}$ (b) $e^{\sec^2(4x)}$

   (c) $\sin(e^{x^2}) + 4\pi e^{\sqrt{2x}}$ (d) $\ln(4x)^2$

   (e) $\log_e \sqrt{5x} + \cos^2(5x)$

   (f) $\ln(\cos^2 x + 4\pi x)$ (g) $2e^{\frac{x^2}{4}} + 3\ln\left(\dfrac{2x}{5}\right)$

   (h) $\ln(\sin(2x))$ (i) $\sin(e^{5x}) + \cot(e^{-5x})$

2. Find $f'(x)$ of the following:

(a) $f(x) = \dfrac{5}{2e^{4x} + 3}$

(b) $f(x) = 4x^3 e^{x^2}$

(c) $f(x) = \sin^2 x \cdot e^{\cos^2 x}$

(d) $f(x) = \dfrac{1}{\sqrt{\ln(4x) + 3}}$

(e) $f(x) = \ln\sqrt{2x} \cdot \cot^2 x$

(f) $f(x) = \cos\left(\dfrac{e^{4x}}{e^{3x} - 2}\right)$

(g) $f(x) = \ln(\pi x)e^{\pi e^{\pi x}}$

(h) $f(x) = \sqrt{2xe^{x^2} + \pi x}$

(i) $f(x) = \dfrac{\pi \ln(\pi x)}{e^{x^2}}$

(j) $f(x) = \log_e((e^x + 4x)(e^{-x} - 4x))$

3. Find:
   (a) the derivative of $y = e\ln(\sqrt{2x})$ at $x = 3$
   (b) the derivative of $y = \sec(\ln(2x))$ at $x = 10$
   (c) the derivative of $y = e^{\sin(\theta)} + 4\ln(\cos\theta)$ at $\theta = 45°$
   (d) $f'(0)$ given that $f(x) = \dfrac{1}{2e^{4x} + 3}$
   (e) $f'\left(\dfrac{1}{4}\right)$ given that $f(x) = e^{4x^2} + 2x\ln(x)$
   (f) $g'(30°)$ given that $g(\theta) = 2e\cos^2(\theta) - 4\csc\left(\dfrac{\theta}{2}\right)$

◆

CHAPTER 4

IMPLICIT DIFFERENTIATION

INTRODUCTION

So far, you have been differentiating functions where the dependent variable y is confined and isolated on the left-hand side (LHS) of the equation while the independent variable x is on the right-hand side (RHS) of the equation. Such functions are known as **explicit functions** where the dependent variable can be expressed in terms of one or more independent variables.

$$y = 4x^2 - 3x + 5 \quad \bullet\!\!\!-\!\!\!\mid \begin{array}{l} y \text{ is the dependent variable and} \\ x \text{ is an independent variable} \end{array}$$

The above function can be denoted as $y = f(x)$ where the dependent variable y is expressed explicitly in terms of the independent variable x. In other words, the y value is the subject of the formula and varies according to the x value.

Differentiating an explicit function is quite straightforward and many examples come to mind, such as,

$$y = 2x^2 + \sin x + e^{x^2}$$
$$\frac{dy}{dx} = 4x + \cos x + 2xe^{x^2} \qquad \textbf{[Result (4.1)]}$$

However, suppose you were asked to differentiate $x^2 + y^2 = 1$ or $x^2 + xy + y^2 = 16$. How would you do this? These functions are examples of **implicit functions** where the dependent variable is not "explicitly" defined in terms of the independent variable. In other words, it is a function in which the dependent variable cannot be expressed in terms of some independent variables. An implicit function is usually given in terms of both dependent and independent variables and it can be denoted as $f(x, y) = 0$. You could try to rearrange the implicit function to obtain an explicit function, but it is often much simpler to leave it as it is and directly apply the technique of implicit differentiation.

Consider the implicit function $x^2 + y^2 - 16 = 0$. Differentiating this function, you have

$$\frac{d}{dx}(x^2) + \frac{d}{dx}(y^2) - \frac{d}{dx}(16) = \frac{d}{dx}(0)$$

Differentiating x^2 will produce $2x$, and differentiating the constants 16 and 0 will each produce 0. So, you now have

$$2x + \frac{d}{dx}(y^2) - 0 = 0$$

 NOTE

The Chain Rule, the Product Rule and the Quotient Rule can be applied to implicit functions.

Then, what about y^2? You can use the Chain Rule.

$$\frac{d}{dx}(y^2) = \frac{d}{dy}(y^2) \cdot \frac{dy}{dx}$$

$$= 2y\frac{dy}{dx}$$

Differentiating in this way is called **implicit differentiation** as opposed to the explicit differentiation in Result (4.1). Therefore, differentiating $x^2 + y^2 - 16 = 0$ implicitly with respect to x would produce

$$2x + 2y\frac{dy}{dx} = 0$$

$$2y\frac{dy}{dx} = -2x$$

$$\frac{dy}{dx} = -\frac{x}{y}$$

Now, let us differentiate $x^2 + xy + y^2 = 16$ with respect to x. You will have

$$\frac{d}{dx}(x^2) + \frac{d}{dx}(xy) + \frac{d}{dx}(y^2) = \frac{d}{dx}(16)$$

$$2x + \frac{d}{dx}(xy) + 2y\frac{dy}{dx} = 0 \quad \bullet\!\!-\!\!-\!\!-\!\!\Big|$$ The derivative of $\frac{d}{dx}(y^2)$ was shown in the previous example

Then, you have

$$\frac{d}{dx}(xy) = x \cdot \frac{d}{dx}(y) + y \cdot \frac{d}{dx}(x) \bullet \longrightarrow \text{ Using the Product Rule}$$

$$= x \cdot 1 \frac{dy}{dx} + y \cdot 1$$

$$= x \frac{dy}{dx} + y$$

Therefore, you have

$$2x + x\frac{dy}{dx} + y + 2y\frac{dy}{dx} = 0$$

$$x\frac{dy}{dx} + 2y\frac{dy}{dx} = -2x - y \bullet \longrightarrow \text{ Leave } \frac{dy}{dx} \text{ on the LHS}$$

$$(x + 2y)\frac{dy}{dx} = -(2x + y) \bullet \longrightarrow \text{ Extract the common factor } \frac{dy}{dx}$$

$$\frac{dy}{dx} = -\frac{(2x + y)}{(x + 2y)} \bullet \longrightarrow \text{ Bring } x + 2y \text{ to the RHS}$$

EXAMPLE 1

Differentiate implicitly $4x^2 - x - 2xy^2 = 1$ with respect to x.

Solution:

$$4x^2 - x - 2xy^2 = 1$$

$$8x - 1 - 2x \cdot 2y\frac{dy}{dx} - y^2 \cdot 2 = 0 \quad \bullet \longrightarrow \quad \text{Applying the Product Rule to the term } 2xy^2$$

$$8x - 1 - 4xy\frac{dy}{dx} - 2y^2 = 0$$

$$-4xy\frac{dy}{dx} = 2y^2 + 1 - 8x$$

$$\frac{dy}{dx} = \frac{\mathbf{2y^2 + 1 - 8x}}{\mathbf{-4xy}}$$

TIP

When moving the term –4xy to the RHS, students often confuse the –ve multiplication with a subtraction, and get the incorrect result of:

$$\frac{dy}{dx} = 2y^2 + 1 - 8x + 4xy \qquad ,$$

EXAMPLE 2

Find $\dfrac{dy}{dx}$ if $\pi \sin x + \dfrac{\sqrt{y}}{e\pi} = 1.$

Solution:

Differentiating implicitly, you have

$$\pi \cos x + \frac{\frac{1}{2}y^{-\frac{1}{2}}}{e\pi}\frac{dy}{dx} = 0$$

$$\frac{\frac{dy}{dx}}{2e\pi\sqrt{y}} = -\pi \cos x$$

$$\frac{dy}{dx} = -2e\pi^2 \sqrt{y} \cos x$$

EXAMPLE 3

Find $\dfrac{dy}{dx}$ if $\sqrt{2x} + \sqrt{2y} = 1$.

Solution:

Differentiating implicitly produces

$$\frac{1}{2}(2x)^{-\frac{1}{2}} \cdot 2 + \frac{1}{2}(2y)^{-\frac{1}{2}} \cdot 2\frac{dy}{dx} = 0$$

$$\frac{1}{\sqrt{2x}} + \frac{1}{\sqrt{2y}}\frac{dy}{dx} = 0$$

$$\frac{1}{\sqrt{2y}}\frac{dy}{dx} = -\frac{1}{\sqrt{2x}}$$

$$\frac{dy}{dx} = -\frac{1}{\sqrt{2x}} \times \sqrt{2y}$$

$$\frac{dy}{dx} = -\sqrt{\frac{y}{x}}$$

EXAMPLE 4

Differentiate implicitly $y^2 + \sqrt{x}y^3 = 4 - xy^2$ with respect to x.

Solution:

$$y^2 + \sqrt{x}y^3 = 4 - xy^2$$

$$2y\frac{dy}{dx} + \sqrt{x}\,3y^2\frac{dy}{dx} + y^3 \cdot \frac{1}{2}x^{-\frac{1}{2}} = 0 - x \cdot 2y\frac{dy}{dx} - y^2 \cdot 1$$

$$2y\frac{dy}{dx} + 3\sqrt{x}\,y^2\frac{dy}{dx} + \frac{y^3}{2\sqrt{x}} = -2xy\frac{dy}{dx} - y^2$$

$$2y\frac{dy}{dx} + 3\sqrt{x}y^2\frac{dy}{dx} + 2xy\frac{dy}{dx} = -y^2 - \frac{y^3}{2\sqrt{x}}$$

$$(2y + 3\sqrt{x}y^2 + 2xy)\frac{dy}{dx} = -y^2 - \frac{y^3}{2\sqrt{x}}$$

$$\frac{dy}{dx} = \frac{-y^2 - \dfrac{y^3}{2\sqrt{x}}}{2y + 3\sqrt{x}y^2 + 2xy}$$

EXAMPLE 5

Differentiate implicitly $x\cos y - \tan y = \dfrac{x^2}{2}$ with respect to x.

Solution:

Differentiating implicitly produces

$$x \cdot (-\sin y)\frac{dy}{dx} + \cos y \cdot 1 - \sec^2 y\frac{dy}{dx} = x$$

$$-x\sin y\frac{dy}{dx} - \sec^2 y\frac{dy}{dx} = x - \cos y$$

$$(-x\sin y - \sec^2 y)\frac{dy}{dx} = x - \cos y$$

$$\frac{dy}{dx} = \frac{x - \cos y}{-x\sin y - \sec^2 y}$$

EXAMPLE 6

Differentiate implicitly $xy + y\cos x = 1$ with respect to x.

Solution:

$$xy + y\cos x = 1$$

$$x \cdot 1\frac{dy}{dx} + y \cdot 1 + y \cdot (-\sin x) + \cos x \cdot 1\frac{dy}{dx} = 0$$

$$x\frac{dy}{dx} + \cos x\frac{dy}{dx} = y\sin x - y$$

$$(x + \cos x)\frac{dy}{dx} = y\sin x - y$$

$$\frac{dy}{dx} = \frac{y\sin x - y}{x + \cos x}$$

EXAMPLE 7

Differentiate implicitly $x^2y^2 + \ln(y) - \cos(y) = 3x$ with respect to x.

Solution:

$$x^2y^2 + \ln(y) - \cos(y) = 3x$$

$$x^2 \cdot 2y\frac{dy}{dx} + 2x \cdot y^2 + \frac{1}{y}\frac{dy}{dx} - (-\sin(y))\frac{dy}{dx} = 3$$

$$2x^2y\frac{dy}{dx} + 2xy^2 + \frac{1}{y}\frac{dy}{dx} + \sin(y)\frac{dy}{dx} = 3$$

$$2x^2y\frac{dy}{dx} + \frac{1}{y}\frac{dy}{dx} + \sin(y)\frac{dy}{dx} = 3 - 2xy^2$$

$$\left(2x^2y + \frac{1}{y} + \sin(y)\right)\frac{dy}{dx} = 3 - 2xy^2$$

$$\left(\frac{2x^2y^2 + 1 + y\sin(y)}{y}\right)\frac{dy}{dx} = 3 - 2xy^2$$

$$\frac{dy}{dx} = \frac{3y - 2xy^3}{2x^2y^2 + 1 + y\sin(y)}$$

EXAMPLE 8

Differentiate implicitly $4x^2 + 2y = 3\ln(y^2) - 3x$ with respect to x.

Solution:

$$4x^2 + 2y = 3\ln(y^2) - 3x$$

$$8x + 2\frac{dy}{dx} = 3 \cdot \frac{1}{y^2} \cdot 2y\frac{dy}{dx} - 3$$

$$8x + 2\frac{dy}{dx} = \frac{6}{y}\frac{dy}{dx} - 3$$

$$8x + 3 = \frac{6}{y}\frac{dy}{dx} - 2\frac{dy}{dx}$$

$$\frac{6}{y}\frac{dy}{dx} - 2\frac{dy}{dx} = 8x + 3$$

$$\left(\frac{6}{y} - 2\right)\frac{dy}{dx} = 8x + 3$$

$$\left(\frac{6 - 2y}{y}\right)\frac{dy}{dx} = 8x + 3$$

$$\frac{dy}{dx} = \frac{y(8x + 3)}{6 - 2y}$$

EXAMPLE 9

Differentiate implicitly $xy + 4x^2 = 3y^2$ with respect to x and find $\frac{dy}{dx}$ when $x = 1$ and $y = -1$.

Solution:

Differentiating implicitly produces

$$x \cdot 1 \frac{dy}{dx} + y \cdot 1 + 8x = 6y \frac{dy}{dx}$$

$$x \frac{dy}{dx} - 6y \frac{dy}{dx} = -y - 8x$$

$$\frac{dy}{dx}(x - 6y) = -y - 8x$$

$$\frac{dy}{dx} = \frac{-y - 8x}{x - 6y}$$

When $x = 1$ and $y = -1$, $\dfrac{dy}{dx} = \dfrac{-(-1) - 8(1)}{1 - 6(-1)} = -1$

EXAMPLE 10

Differentiate implicitly $x \ln y + 4x^2 = 3y^2 - 4x$ with respect to x and find $\dfrac{dy}{dx}$ when $x = 3$ and $y = 1$.

Solution:

Differentiating implicitly produces

$$x \cdot \frac{1}{y} \frac{dy}{dx} + \ln y \cdot 1 + 8x = 6y \frac{dy}{dx} - 4$$

$$\frac{x}{y} \frac{dy}{dx} + \ln y + 8x = 6y \frac{dy}{dx} - 4$$

$$\frac{x}{y}\frac{dy}{dx} - 6y\frac{dy}{dx} = -4 - \ln y - 8x$$

$$\left(\frac{x}{y} - 6y\right)\frac{dy}{dx} = -4 - \ln y - 8x$$

$$\left(\frac{x - 6y^2}{y}\right)\frac{dy}{dx} = -4 - \ln y - 8x$$

$$\frac{dy}{dx} = \frac{y(-4 - \ln y - 8x)}{x - 6y^2}$$

When $x = 3$ and $y = 1$, $\dfrac{dy}{dx} = \dfrac{1(-4 - \ln(1) - 8(3))}{3 - 6(1)^2} = \dfrac{28}{3}$

EXAMPLE 11

Differentiate implicitly $\dfrac{x}{y} = 3y^2 + 4x^2$ with respect to x and find $\dfrac{dy}{dx}$ at the point $(5, 5)$.

Solution:

Differentiating implicitly produces

$$\frac{y \cdot 1 - x \cdot 1\dfrac{dy}{dx}}{y^2} = 6y\frac{dy}{dx} + 8x$$

$$\frac{y - x\dfrac{dy}{dx}}{y^2} = 6y\frac{dy}{dx} + 8x$$

$$y - x\frac{dy}{dx} = y^2\left(6y\frac{dy}{dx} + 8x\right)$$

$$y - x\frac{dy}{dx} = 6y^3\frac{dy}{dx} + 8xy^2$$

$$-x\frac{dy}{dx} - 6y^3\frac{dy}{dx} = 8xy^2 - y$$

$$(-x - 6y^3)\frac{dy}{dx} = 8xy^2 - y$$

$$\frac{dy}{dx} = \frac{8xy^2 - y}{-x - 6y^3}$$

At point $(5, 5)$, $\dfrac{dy}{dx} = \dfrac{8(5)(5)^2 - (5)}{-(5) - 6(5)^3} = -\dfrac{199}{151}$

EXAMPLE 12

Differentiate implicitly $\dfrac{x}{y} - 4x = 2xy - 3y$ with respect to x and find $\dfrac{dy}{dx}$ at the point $(-2, -2)$.

Solution:

Differentiating implicitly produces

$$\frac{y \cdot 1 - x \cdot 1\frac{dy}{dx}}{y^2} - 4 = 2x \cdot 1\frac{dy}{dx} + y \cdot 2 - 3\frac{dy}{dx}$$

$$\frac{y - x\dfrac{dy}{dx}}{y^2} - 4 = 2x\frac{dy}{dx} + 2y - 3\frac{dy}{dx}$$

$$\frac{y - x\dfrac{dy}{dx}}{y^2} = 2x\frac{dy}{dx} + 2y - 3\frac{dy}{dx} + 4$$

$$y - x\frac{dy}{dx} = y^2\left(2x\frac{dy}{dx} + 2y - 3\frac{dy}{dx} + 4\right)$$

$$y - x\frac{dy}{dx} = 2xy^2\frac{dy}{dx} + 2y^3 - 3y^2\frac{dy}{dx} + 4y^2$$

$$3y^2\frac{dy}{dx} - x\frac{dy}{dx} - 2xy^2\frac{dy}{dx} = 2y^3 - y + 4y^2$$

$$\left(3y^2 - x - 2xy^2\right)\frac{dy}{dx} = 2y^3 - y + 4y^2$$

$$\frac{dy}{dx} = \frac{2y^3 - y + 4y^2}{3y^2 - x - 2xy^2}$$

At point (–2, –2), $\dfrac{dy}{dx} = \dfrac{2(-2)^3 - (-2) + 4(-2)^2}{3(-2)^2 - (-2) - 2(-2)(-2)^2}$

$$= \frac{1}{15}$$

TIP

When substituting negative values into an equation, always use brackets around them so that you will not carelessly overlook the minus sign in your calculations.

REVIEW QUESTIONS

1. Differentiate implicitly the following with respect to x:

   (a) $2xy - 4x = 3y^2$

   (b) $3xy^2 - 3 = 2x + 4y$

   (c) $10x^3 - 5y^2 = \dfrac{xy}{5}$

   (d) $\dfrac{2x}{y} + 3x = 4y^5$

   (e) $5y^2 - 2\dfrac{x}{y} = 4x^3$

   (f) $\dfrac{x}{y} + x^2y = 4x - 3y$

   (g) $2x^3 - \dfrac{5}{y^2} = 4xy - 2x^7$

   (h) $\dfrac{x}{y} = 4x^3 - 2xy^2$

2. Find the implicit derivatives of the following with respect to x:

   (a) $\sqrt{5x} = e\pi x - \sqrt{5y}$

   (b) $2x \sin y = \dfrac{3x^2}{4} + e \cos y$

   (c) $\sin x + 4y = \dfrac{\sqrt{y}}{2e\pi}$

   (d) $\dfrac{\sin x}{xy} = 4 \cos y$

   (e) $\dfrac{4y - \cos y}{x^3} = 1$

   (f) $e^y \cos x + xy = \ln x$

   (g) $\ln(y^2) - 3 \cos x = 4 \tan y + 2e^{4x}$

3. Evaluate the following:

   (a) Given $xy + y^2 = 2x - 4xy$. Find $\dfrac{dy}{dx}$ when $x = 1$ and $y = 0$.

(b) Given $x^2y + 4y^3 = \dfrac{xy}{5}$. Find $\dfrac{dy}{dx}$ when $x = 2$ and $y = -2$.

(c) Given $x^3y = 5xy - 4$. Find $\dfrac{dy}{dx}$ when $x = 1$ and $y = 1$.

(d) Given $\dfrac{2x}{y} + y^3 = 5xy - 4x$. Find $\dfrac{dy}{dx}$ when $x = 3$ and $y = -2$.

4. Solve the following:

(a) Differentiate implicitly $4x^2 - 3xy = \dfrac{1}{y}$ with respect to x and find $\dfrac{dy}{dx}$ at point $(1, 1)$.

(b) Differentiate implicitly $x^2 - x^3 = y^5 + y^4$ with respect to x and find $\dfrac{dy}{dx}$ at point $(-1, 1)$.

(c) Differentiate implicitly $3y^2 - 4x^2 = xy$ with respect to x and find $\dfrac{dy}{dx}$ at point $\left(1, \dfrac{4}{3}\right)$.

(d) Differentiate implicitly $\dfrac{y}{x} + 4xy = 3x^3 + \ln(x)$ with respect to x and find $\dfrac{dy}{dx}$ at point $(2, 1)$.

CHAPTER 5

PARTIAL DERIVATIVES

INTRODUCTION

Thus far, you have been dealing mainly with functions of only one variable, usually x. Nevertheless, in the fields of engineering and the natural sciences, you often have to deal with functions of several variables, typically two or even three, such as $f(x, y, z)$. In such cases, when you need to differentiate with respect to x, for instance, you would treat y and z as constants. The following examples will illustrate the technique of **partial differentiation**.

EXAMPLE 1

If $w = y^2 + \dfrac{x}{y} + \dfrac{x^2}{3}$, find $\dfrac{\partial w}{\partial x}$ and $\dfrac{\partial w}{\partial y}$.

Solution:

First, let us become familiar with the notation used in partial derivatives. You already know that the notation $\dfrac{dy}{dx}$ refers to a total differential. However, when you are dealing with functions containing more than one variable, the derivative is represented by **partial derivatives,** such as $\dfrac{\partial w}{\partial x}$ or $\dfrac{\partial w}{\partial y}$.

> **NOTE**
>
> The letter d in $\dfrac{dy}{dx}$ is pronounced as 'dee' while the Greek letter ∂, pronounced as 'del' (short for 'delta'), is used to distinguish partial derivatives from ordinary derivatives.

Partial derivatives allow you to see how the function changes if you let one of those variables change while the others remain fixed.

$$w = y^2 + \frac{x}{y} + \frac{x^2}{3}$$

$$\frac{\partial w}{\partial x} = 0 + \frac{1}{y} + \frac{2x}{3}$$

Observe that you treat y as a constant when you are differentiating with respect to x

$$= \frac{1}{y} + \frac{2}{3}x$$

$$\frac{\partial w}{\partial y} = 2y + x\left(-y^{-2}\right) + 0$$

Observe that you treat x as a constant when you are differentiating with respect to y

$$= 2y - \frac{x}{y^2}$$

Basically, the partial derivative $\dfrac{\partial}{\partial x}$ operates in a similar manner to $\dfrac{d}{dx}$ except that in partial differentiation, you treat other variables as constants.

EXAMPLE 2

Find $\dfrac{\partial z}{\partial x}$ and $\dfrac{\partial z}{\partial y}$ if

(a) $z = x^2 + y^2\sqrt{x} - \dfrac{x^3}{y^3}$

(b) $z = x^2y + y^{\frac{3}{2}} - 3x^3$

Solution:

(a) $\quad z = x^2 + y^2\sqrt{x} - \dfrac{x^3}{y^3}$

$\dfrac{\partial z}{\partial x} = 2x + y^2\left(\dfrac{1}{2}x^{-\frac{1}{2}}\right) - \dfrac{1}{y^3}\left(3x^2\right)$

$\qquad = 2x + \dfrac{y^2}{2\sqrt{x}} - \dfrac{3x^2}{y^3}$

$\dfrac{\partial z}{\partial y} = 0 + 2y\sqrt{x} - x^3\left(-3y^{-4}\right)$

$\qquad = 2y\sqrt{x} + \dfrac{3x^3}{y^4}$

(b) $\quad z = x^2y + y^{\frac{3}{2}} - 3x^3$

$$\frac{\partial z}{\partial x} = y(2x) + 0 - 9x^2$$

$$= 2xy - 9x^2$$

$$\frac{\partial z}{\partial y} = x^2(1) + \frac{3}{2}y^{\frac{1}{2}} - 0$$

$$= x^2 + \frac{3\sqrt{y}}{2}$$

EXAMPLE 3

If $w = (x + y)(3x + y^2)$, how do you find $\dfrac{\partial w}{\partial x}$ and $\dfrac{\partial w}{\partial y}$?

Solution:

This requires the use of the Product Rule.

$$w = \underbrace{(x + y)}_{u}\underbrace{(3x + y^2)}_{v}$$

$$\frac{\partial w}{\partial x} = u\frac{\partial v}{\partial x} + v\frac{\partial u}{\partial x}$$

$$= (x + y)(3 + 0) + (3x + y^2)(1 + 0)$$
$$= 3(x + y) + 3x + y^2$$

$$= 3x + 3y + 3x + y^2$$
$$= \mathbf{6x + y^2 + 3y}$$

$$\frac{\partial w}{\partial y} = u\frac{\partial v}{\partial y} + v\frac{\partial u}{\partial y}$$

$$= (x + y)(0 + 2y) + (3x + y^2)(0 + 1)$$
$$= 2y(x + y) + 3x + y^2$$
$$= 2xy + 2y^2 + 3x + y^2$$
$$= \mathbf{2xy + 3y^2 + 3x}$$

EXAMPLE 4

' If $w = (2x - 4y)(5y - 3x)$, find $\dfrac{\partial w}{\partial x}$ and $\dfrac{\partial w}{\partial y}$.

Solution:

Once again, you can resort to the Product Rule.

$$w = \underbrace{(2x - 4y)}_{u}\underbrace{(5y - 3x)}_{v}$$

$$\frac{\partial w}{\partial x} = (2x - 4y)(0 - 3) + (5y - 3x)(2 - 0)$$
$$= -3(2x - 4y) + 2(5y - 3x)$$
$$= -6x + 12y + 10y - 6x$$
$$= \mathbf{22y - 12x}$$

$$\frac{\partial w}{\partial y} = (2x - 4y)(5 - 0) + (5y - 3x)(0 - 4)$$
$$= 5(2x - 4y) - 4(5y - 3x)$$
$$= 10x - 20y - 20y + 12x$$
$$= \mathbf{22x - 40y}$$

EXAMPLE 5

If $z = \dfrac{x + 2y}{2x - y}$, find $\dfrac{\partial z}{\partial x}$ and $\dfrac{\partial z}{\partial y}$.

Solution:

You now need to use the Quotient Rule.

$$z = \frac{x + 2y}{2x - y} \begin{matrix} \}u \\ \}v \end{matrix}$$

$$\frac{\partial z}{\partial x} = \frac{v\dfrac{\partial u}{\partial x} - u\dfrac{\partial v}{\partial x}}{v^2}$$

$$= \frac{(2x - y)(1 + 0) - (x + 2y)(2 - 0)}{(2x - y)^2}$$

$$= \frac{(2x - y) - 2(x + 2y)}{(2x - y)^2}$$

$$= \frac{2x - y - 2x - 4y}{(2x - y)^2}$$

$$= -\frac{5y}{(2x - y)^2}$$

$$\frac{\partial z}{\partial y} = \frac{v\dfrac{\partial u}{\partial y} - u\dfrac{\partial v}{\partial y}}{v^2}$$

$$= \frac{(2x - y)(0 + 2) - (x + 2y)(0 - 1)}{(2x - y)^2}$$

$$= \frac{2(2x - y) + 1(x + 2y)}{(2x - y)^2}$$

$$= \frac{4x - 2y + x + 2y}{(2x - y)^2}$$

$$= \frac{5x}{(2x - y)^2}$$

EXAMPLE 6

If $z = \dfrac{2x + 2y}{x - \sqrt{y}}$, find $\dfrac{\partial z}{\partial x}$ and $\dfrac{\partial z}{\partial y}$.

Solution:

You can use the Quotient Rule.

$$z = \frac{2x + 2y \quad \}u}{x - \sqrt{y} \quad \}v}$$

$$\frac{\partial z}{\partial x} = \frac{v\dfrac{\partial u}{\partial x} - u\dfrac{\partial v}{\partial x}}{v^2}$$

$$= \frac{(x - \sqrt{y})(2 + 0) - (2x + 2y)(1 - 0)}{(x - \sqrt{y})^2}$$

$$= \frac{2(x - \sqrt{y}) - (2x + 2y)}{(x - \sqrt{y})^2}$$

$$= \frac{2x - 2\sqrt{y} - 2x - 2y}{(x - \sqrt{y})^2}$$

$$= \frac{-2\sqrt{y} - 2y}{(x - \sqrt{y})^2}$$

$$= \frac{-2(\sqrt{y} + y)}{(x - \sqrt{y})^2}$$

$$\frac{\partial z}{\partial y} = \frac{v\dfrac{\partial u}{\partial y} - u\dfrac{\partial v}{\partial y}}{v^2}$$

$$= \frac{(x - \sqrt{y})(0 + 2) - (2x + 2y)\left(0 - \frac{1}{2}y^{-\frac{1}{2}}\right)}{(x - \sqrt{y})^2}$$

$$= \frac{2(x - \sqrt{y}) - \left(-\frac{1}{2\sqrt{y}}\right)(2x + 2y)}{(x - \sqrt{y})^2}$$

$$= \frac{2x - 2\sqrt{y} + \frac{2x}{2\sqrt{y}} + \frac{2y}{2\sqrt{y}}}{(x - \sqrt{y})^2}$$

$$= \frac{2x - 2\sqrt{y} + \frac{x}{\sqrt{y}} + \frac{y}{\sqrt{y}}}{(x - \sqrt{y})^2}$$

$$= \frac{\frac{2x\sqrt{y}}{\sqrt{y}} - \frac{2\sqrt{y} \cdot \sqrt{y}}{\sqrt{y}} + \frac{x}{\sqrt{y}} + \frac{y}{\sqrt{y}}}{(x - \sqrt{y})^2}$$

$$= \frac{2x\sqrt{y} - 2y + x + y}{\sqrt{y}(x - \sqrt{y})^2}$$

$$= \frac{2x\sqrt{y} + x - y}{\sqrt{y}(x - \sqrt{y})^2}$$

Now, let us deal with partial derivatives involving trigonometric functions.

EXAMPLE 7

If $w = \cos(8x - y)$, find $\dfrac{\partial w}{\partial x}$ and $\dfrac{\partial w}{\partial y}$.

Solution:

$$\frac{\partial w}{\partial x} = -\sin(8x - y)(8 - 0)$$

$$= -8\,\sin(8x - y)$$

$$\frac{\partial w}{\partial y} = -\sin(8x - y)(0 - 1)$$

$$= \sin(8x - y)$$

EXAMPLE 8

Find $\dfrac{\partial z}{\partial x}$ and $\dfrac{\partial z}{\partial y}$ if

(a) $z = \tan(\sqrt{2x} + y^2)$ 　　　(b) $z = \dfrac{\cos(8x - y)}{2xy^2}$

(c) $z = \cos(x + y)\sin(x - y)$

Solution:

(a) $z = \tan(\sqrt{2x} + y^2)$

$$\frac{\partial z}{\partial x} = \sec^2(\sqrt{2x} + y^2) \cdot \frac{\partial}{\partial x}(\sqrt{2x} + y^2)$$

$$= \sec^2(\sqrt{2x} + y^2) \times \left[\frac{1}{2}(2x)^{-\frac{1}{2}} \cdot 2 + 0 \right]$$

$$= \frac{1}{\sqrt{2x}} \sec^2(\sqrt{2x} + y^2)$$

Observe the use of the Chain Rule in the second stage of the differentiation

$$\frac{\partial z}{\partial y} = \sec^2(\sqrt{2x} + y^2) \cdot \frac{\partial}{\partial y}(\sqrt{2x} + y^2)$$

$$= \sec^2(\sqrt{2x} + y^2) \cdot 2y$$

$$= 2y \, \sec^2(\sqrt{2x} + y^2)$$

(b) $z = \dfrac{\cos(8x - y)}{2xy^2} \begin{matrix} \}u \\ \}v \end{matrix}$

$$\frac{\partial z}{\partial x} = \frac{v \dfrac{\partial u}{\partial x} - u \dfrac{\partial v}{\partial x}}{v^2}$$

$$= \frac{2xy^2 \cdot (-\sin(8x - y)) \cdot 8 - \cos(8x - y) \cdot 2y^2}{(2xy^2)^2}$$

$$= \frac{-16xy^2 \sin(8x - y) - 2y^2 \cos(8x - y)}{4x^2y^4}$$

$$\frac{\partial z}{\partial y} = \frac{v\dfrac{\partial u}{\partial y} - u\dfrac{\partial v}{\partial y}}{v^2}$$

$$= \frac{2xy^2 \cdot (-\sin(8x - y)) \cdot (-1) - \cos(8x - y) \cdot 4xy}{(2xy^2)^2}$$

$$= \frac{-2xy^2 \sin(8x - y) - 4xy \cos(8x - y)}{4x^2y^4}$$

(c) $z = \underbrace{\cos(x + y)}_{u}\underbrace{\sin(x - y)}_{v}$

$$\frac{\partial z}{\partial x} = u\frac{\partial v}{\partial x} + v\frac{\partial u}{\partial x}$$

$$= \cos(x + y) \cos(x - y) \cdot (1 - 0) +$$
$$\sin(x - y) \cdot (-\sin(x + y)) \cdot (1 + 0)$$

$$= \cos(x + y) \cos(x - y) - \sin(x + y) \sin(x - y)$$

Let $a = x + y$ and $b = x - y$. Then,

$$\frac{\partial z}{\partial x} = \cos(a) \cos(b) - \sin(a) \sin(b)$$

$$= \cos(a + b) \quad \bullet\!\!-\!\!-\!\!-\!\!-\!\!-\!\!| \text{ Sum-Difference formula}$$

$$= \cos((x + y) + (x - y))$$

$$= \mathbf{cos(2x)}$$

$$\frac{\partial z}{\partial y} = u\frac{\partial v}{\partial y} + v\frac{\partial u}{\partial y}$$

$$= \cos(x + y) \cos(x - y) \cdot (0 - 1) +$$
$$\quad \sin(x - y) \cdot (-\sin(x + y)) \cdot (0 + 1)$$

$$= -\cos(x + y) \cos(x - y) - \sin(x + y) \sin(x - y)$$

$$= -(\cos(x + y) \cos(x - y) + \sin(x + y) \sin(x - y))$$

Again, let $a = x + y$ and $b = x - y$. Then

$$\frac{\partial z}{\partial y} = -(\cos(a) \cos(b) + \sin(a) \sin(b))$$

$$= -\cos(a - b) \quad \bullet\!\!-\!\!-\!\!-\!\!| \text{ Sum-Difference formula}$$

$$= -\cos((x + y) - (x - y))$$

$$= \mathbf{-cos(2y)}$$

Next, let us move on to partial derivatives involving exponential functions.

EXAMPLE 9

If $z = e^{x^2+y^2}$, find an expression for $\dfrac{\partial z}{\partial x} + \dfrac{\partial z}{\partial y}$.

Solution:

$$\frac{\partial z}{\partial x} = e^{x^2+y^2} \cdot \frac{\partial}{\partial x}(x^2 + y^2)$$

$$= 2xe^{x^2+y^2}$$

$$\frac{\partial z}{\partial y} = e^{x^2+y^2} \cdot \frac{\partial}{\partial y}(x^2 + y^2)$$

$$= 2ye^{x^2+y^2}$$

Therefore, $\dfrac{\partial z}{\partial x} + \dfrac{\partial z}{\partial y} = 2xe^{x^2+y^2} + 2ye^{x^2+y^2}$

$$= 2e^{x^2+y^2}(x + y)$$

EXAMPLE 10

If $w = \dfrac{e^x + e^y}{e^x - e^y}$, show that $\dfrac{\partial w}{\partial x} + \dfrac{\partial w}{\partial y} = 0$.

Solution:

$$w = \frac{e^x + e^y \}u}{e^x - e^y \}v}$$

$$\frac{\partial w}{\partial x} = \frac{(e^x - e^y)\cdot(e^x \cdot 1) - (e^x + e^y) \cdot e^x \cdot 1}{(e^x - e^y)^2}$$

$$= \frac{e^{2x} - e^{x+y} - e^{2x} - e^{x+y}}{(e^x - e^y)^2}$$

$$= -\frac{2e^{x+y}}{(e^x - e^y)^2}$$

$$\frac{\partial w}{\partial y} = \frac{(e^x - e^y)\cdot(e^y \cdot 1) - (e^x + e^y) \cdot (-e^y \cdot 1)}{(e^x - e^y)^2}$$

$$= \frac{e^{x+y} - e^{2y} + e^{2y} + e^{x+y}}{(e^x - e^y)^2}$$

$$= \frac{2e^{x+y}}{(e^x - e^y)^2}$$

Therefore, $\dfrac{\partial w}{\partial x} + \dfrac{\partial w}{\partial y} = -\dfrac{2e^{x+y}}{(e^x - e^y)^2} + \dfrac{2e^{x+y}}{(e^x - e^y)^2} = \mathbf{0}$ (As required)

EXAMPLE 11

If $V = f(x^2 + y^2 + z^2)$, find an expression for $x\dfrac{\partial V}{\partial y} + y\dfrac{\partial V}{\partial x}$.

Solution:

Here, V is a function of $(x^2 + y^2 + z^2)$ but the exact function is not known. You can treat this as a composite function and represent the derivative of the function with respect to its own combined variable $\left(x^2 + y^2 + z^2\right)$ as $f'\left(x^2 + y^2 + z^2\right)$.

$$V = f\left(x^2 + y^2 + z^2\right)$$

$$\frac{\partial V}{\partial x} = f'\left(x^2 + y^2 + z^2\right) \cdot 2x \qquad \frac{\partial V}{\partial y} = f'\left(x^2 + y^2 + z^2\right) \cdot 2y$$

$$= 2xf'\left(x^2 + y^2 + z^2\right) \qquad\qquad = 2yf'\left(x^2 + y^2 + z^2\right)$$

Therefore, $x\dfrac{\partial V}{\partial y} + y\dfrac{\partial V}{\partial x}$

$$= 2xyf'\left(x^2 + y^2 + z^2\right) + 2yxf'\left(x^2 + y^2 + z^2\right)$$

$$= \mathbf{4xyf'\left(x^2 + y^2 + z^2\right)}$$

You have been using the standard Chain Rule for functions of one variable. You can extend the Chain Rule to multivariable functions in partial differentiation.

Suppose z is a function of two variables, x and y; and x and y are both functions of two variables, r and θ. In function notation, you have

$$z = f(x, y) \text{ where } x = g(r, \theta) \text{ and } y = h(r, \theta)$$

Then, in this case, the Chain Rule can be written as:

$$\frac{\partial z}{\partial r} = \frac{\partial z}{\partial x} \frac{\partial x}{\partial r} + \frac{\partial z}{\partial y} \frac{\partial y}{\partial r}$$

$$\frac{\partial z}{\partial \theta} = \frac{\partial z}{\partial x} \frac{\partial x}{\partial \theta} + \frac{\partial z}{\partial y} \frac{\partial y}{\partial \theta}$$

EXAMPLE 12

Use the Chain Rule to obtain $\dfrac{\partial z}{\partial r}$ and $\dfrac{\partial z}{\partial \theta}$ given that

$$z = x^3 + 2xy + y^2 \text{ and } \begin{matrix} x = r \cos \theta \\ y = r \sin \theta \end{matrix}$$

Solution:

From $z = x^3 + 2xy + y^2$, you have

$$\frac{\partial z}{\partial x} = 3x^2 + 2y \qquad\qquad \frac{\partial z}{\partial y} = 2x + 2y$$

From $x = r \cos \theta$,   From $y = r \sin \theta$,

$$\frac{\partial x}{\partial r} = \cos \theta \qquad\qquad \frac{\partial y}{\partial r} = \sin \theta$$

$$\frac{\partial x}{\partial \theta} = -r \sin \theta \qquad\qquad \frac{\partial y}{\partial \theta} = r \cos \theta$$

Therefore, using the Chain Rule for partial differentiation,

$$\frac{\partial z}{\partial r} = \frac{\partial z}{\partial x} \cdot \frac{\partial x}{\partial r} + \frac{\partial z}{\partial y} \cdot \frac{\partial y}{\partial r}$$

$$= (3x^2 + 2y)\cos\theta + (2x + 2y)\sin\theta$$

$$\frac{\partial z}{\partial \theta} = \frac{\partial z}{\partial x} \cdot \frac{\partial x}{\partial \theta} + \frac{\partial z}{\partial y} \cdot \frac{\partial y}{\partial \theta}$$

$$= -r(3x^2 + 2y)\sin\theta + r(2x + 2y)\cos\theta$$

$$= r\{(2x + 2y)\cos\theta - (3x^2 + 2y)\sin\theta\}$$

EXAMPLE 13

If $w = \dfrac{1}{x^2 + y^2 + z^2}$, show that $x\dfrac{\partial w}{\partial x} + y\dfrac{\partial w}{\partial y} + z\dfrac{\partial w}{\partial z} = -2w$.

Solution:

$$w = \frac{1}{x^2 + y^2 + z^2} = \left(x^2 + y^2 + z^2\right)^{-1}$$

$$\frac{\partial w}{\partial x} = -1 \cdot \left(x^2 + y^2 + z^2\right)^{-2} \cdot 2x = -\frac{2x}{\left(x^2 + y^2 + z^2\right)^2}$$

Similarly,

$$\frac{\partial w}{\partial y} = -\frac{2y}{\left(x^2 + y^2 + z^2\right)^2} \quad \text{and} \quad \frac{\partial w}{\partial z} = -\frac{2z}{\left(x^2 + y^2 + z^2\right)^2}$$

Therefore,

$$x\frac{\partial w}{\partial x} + y\frac{\partial w}{\partial y} + z\frac{\partial w}{\partial z}$$

$$= \frac{-2x^2}{\left(x^2 + y^2 + z^2\right)^2} + \frac{-2y^2}{\left(x^2 + y^2 + z^2\right)^2} + \frac{-2z^2}{\left(x^2 + y^2 + z^2\right)^2}$$

$$= \frac{-2(x^2 + y^2 + z^2)}{\left(x^2 + y^2 + z^2\right)^2}$$

$$= -\frac{2}{x^2 + y^2 + z^2}$$

$$= -2 \cdot \frac{1}{x^2 + y^2 + z^2} = -2w \quad \text{(As required)}$$

EXAMPLE 14

Show that if $V = \sqrt{(x^2 + y^2)}$, then $\dfrac{\partial V}{\partial x} + \dfrac{\partial V}{\partial y} = \dfrac{x + y}{V}$.

Solution:

$$V = \sqrt{(x^2 + y^2)} = (x^2 + y^2)^{\frac{1}{2}}$$

$$\frac{\partial V}{\partial x} = \frac{1}{2}(x^2 + y^2)^{-\frac{1}{2}} \cdot 2x \qquad \frac{\partial V}{\partial y} = \frac{1}{2}(x^2 + y^2)^{-\frac{1}{2}} \cdot 2y$$

$$= \frac{x}{\sqrt{x^2 + y^2}} \qquad\qquad\qquad = \frac{y}{\sqrt{x^2 + y^2}}$$

Therefore, $\dfrac{\partial V}{\partial x} + \dfrac{\partial V}{\partial y} = \dfrac{x}{\sqrt{x^2 + y^2}} + \dfrac{y}{\sqrt{x^2 + y^2}}$

$$= \frac{x + y}{\sqrt{x^2 + y^2}} = \frac{x + y}{V} \quad \text{(As required)}$$

REVIEW QUESTIONS

1. Find $\dfrac{\partial z}{\partial x}$ and $\dfrac{\partial z}{\partial y}$ for each of the following functions:

   (a) $z = x^3 + 4y^2 - 3x^2 y$

   (b) $z = \dfrac{2x}{3y} + 4x^2 + \dfrac{12y}{7}$

   (c) $z = \sqrt{x}y^2 - \sqrt{y}x^2 + \dfrac{x^2}{y^2}$

(d) $z = (4x - 3y^3)(2x^2 - 5y)$

(e) $z = (4x^2 + 2y)(3y^2 - 4x)$

(f) $z = \dfrac{2x + 4y}{3y - 5x}$

(g) $z = \dfrac{4x^2 - 2y^3}{2x + 4y^2}$

(h) $z = \sin(4x^2 - y^3)$

(i) $z = \cos(\sqrt{5x} + \sqrt{3y})$

(j) $z = \dfrac{\sin(2x - 3y)}{3x^2y}$

2. For each of the following, find an expression for $\dfrac{\partial z}{\partial x} + \dfrac{\partial z}{\partial y}$:

(a) $z = 4e^{x^2 - y^2}$ (b) $z = 2xe^{2y}$ (c) $z = \dfrac{3e^{4x}}{\tan 4y}$

3. Prove the following expressions:

(a) If $z = \dfrac{4e^{2x}}{5e^{3y}}$, show that $\dfrac{\partial z}{\partial x} + \dfrac{\partial z}{\partial y} = -z$.

(b) If $z = \dfrac{25e^{2x}}{7e^{2y}}$, show that $\dfrac{\partial z}{\partial x} = -\dfrac{\partial z}{\partial y}$.

(c) If $w = \sqrt{x^2 + y^2 + z^2}$, show that $2\dfrac{\partial w}{\partial x} - \dfrac{\partial w}{\partial z} = \dfrac{2x - z}{w}$.

(d) If $w = \dfrac{2}{3x^3 + 4y^3 + 5y^3}$, show that

$$x\frac{\partial w}{\partial x} + y\frac{\partial w}{\partial y} + z\frac{\partial w}{\partial z} = -6w.$$

4. Find the required expressions:

(a) If $V = f\left(\dfrac{x^3 + y^3}{z^3}\right)$, find $x\dfrac{\partial V}{\partial x} + z\dfrac{\partial V}{\partial z}$.

(b) If $V = f\left(\sqrt{2x} + \sqrt{2y} + \sqrt{2z}\right)$, find $2y\dfrac{\partial V}{\partial x} - 2z\dfrac{\partial V}{\partial z}$.

(c) If $V = f\left(\dfrac{\sqrt{2x} + 3y^2}{z^3}\right)$, find $\sqrt{2x}\,\dfrac{\partial V}{\partial x} + \dfrac{\partial V}{\partial y} + z\dfrac{\partial V}{\partial z}$.

5. Solve the following:

(a) Find $\dfrac{\partial z}{\partial r}$ and $\dfrac{\partial z}{\partial s}$ if $z = 4x^3 - 3y^4$, $x = 2r + 5s$ and $y = rs$.

(b) Find $\dfrac{\partial z}{\partial x}$ and $\dfrac{\partial z}{\partial y}$ if $z = 2r^2 - 4rs + 2s^2$, $r = 4x^2 + 4y^2$ and $s = 4xy^2$.

(c) Find $\dfrac{\partial z}{\partial r}$ and $\dfrac{\partial z}{\partial \theta}$ if $z = 4x^2 + 3y^2 + 2x + y$, $x = r^2 \cos\theta$ and $y = r^2 \sin\theta$.

ANSWERS

Chapter 1   Differentiation of Polynomials

1. (a) 3

   (b) $-\dfrac{4}{3x^2}$

   (c) $2x + 4$

   (d) $-\dfrac{1}{(x-4)^2}$

   (e) $\dfrac{1}{\sqrt{2x}}$

   (f) $-\dfrac{1}{2(x+4)^{\frac{3}{2}}}$

   (g) $\dfrac{3}{5}$

   (h) $2x - 5$

2. (a) $6x^2 - 6x + 4$

   (b) $8x + \dfrac{9}{x^4}$

   (c) $\dfrac{3}{2\sqrt{x}} - 8x$

   (d) $4\pi - \dfrac{3}{2x^{\frac{3}{2}}}$

   (e) $4 - \dfrac{3}{x^2}$

   (f) $5x^{\frac{3}{2}} - 6x^{\frac{1}{2}} - \dfrac{3\pi}{2x^{\frac{3}{2}}}$

3. (a) $f'(x) = 56(2x - 3)^6$

   (b) $f'(x) = -\dfrac{30}{(2x + 4)^6}$

   (c) $f'(x) = (18x^2 - 9)(2x^3 - 3x + 2)^2$

(d) $f'(x) = -\dfrac{6x + 2}{(x + 5)^5}$

(e) $f'(x) = (-18x - 9)(x + 3)^4$

(f) $f'(x) = -\dfrac{36x - 36}{(2x^2 - 4x + 5)^3}$

4. (a) $\dfrac{dy}{dx} = (28x^2 - 18x - 16)(x^2 - 4)^2$

(b) $\dfrac{dy}{dx} = 4\pi\left(\sqrt{x + 3}\right) + \dfrac{4\pi x + 5}{2\sqrt{x + 3}}$

(c) $\dfrac{dy}{dx} = 28x^3 - 54x^2 + 20x + 12$

(d) $\dfrac{dy}{dx} = \dfrac{\sqrt{x} + 4}{\sqrt{2x}} + \dfrac{\sqrt{2x} - 3}{2\sqrt{x}}$

(e) $\dfrac{dy}{dx} = \dfrac{1}{(4x + 3)^2}$ (f) $\dfrac{dy}{dx} = \dfrac{-24x^2 - 80x + 6}{(4x^2 + 3)^3}$

(g) $\dfrac{dy}{dx} = \dfrac{(x^2 - 3)^3 - 3(x + 4)}{2\sqrt{x + 4}(x^2 - 3)^{\frac{5}{2}}}$

(h) $\dfrac{dy}{dx} = \dfrac{24x^2 - 16}{(x^3 - 2x + 4)^2}$

(i) $\dfrac{dy}{dx} = \dfrac{-5\sqrt{3x} - 12\pi\sqrt{x}}{2\sqrt{3x^2}\left(\sqrt{3x} - 5\right)^2}$

Chapter 2   Differentiation of Trigonometric Functions

1. (a) $8\pi \cos(4x - 3)$

   (b) $-10\pi \sec^2(5 - 2x)$

   (c) $-\dfrac{3\pi}{5} \sin(3x + 2\pi)$

   (d) $2\pi^2 \sec\left(\pi x - \dfrac{3}{\pi}\right) \tan\left(\pi x - \dfrac{3}{\pi}\right)$

   (e) $-12 \cot(3x + 2\pi)\, \mathrm{cosec}(3x + 2\pi)$

   (f) $-6 \, \mathrm{cosec}^2\left(\dfrac{\pi}{6} - 2\pi x\right)$

   (g) $-18\pi x \cot(3x^2 + 4\pi)\, \mathrm{cosec}(3x^2 + 4\pi)$

2. (a) $f'(x) = 4 \sin(2\pi x) + 8\pi x \cos(2\pi x)$

   (b) $f'(x) = -\dfrac{6}{x} \sin(3x + 4\pi) - \dfrac{2}{x^2} \cos(3x + 4\pi)$

   (c) $f'(x) = -60\pi \cot^2(4x)\, \mathrm{cosec}^2(4x)$

   (d) $120x^2 \cdot \sec^2(4x^3) \tan(4x^3)$

   (e) $f'(x) = 2 \cos^3 x \cdot \sec^2 x \cdot \tan x - 3 \cos^2 x \cdot \sin x \cdot \tan^2 x$

   (f) $-2\pi^{\frac{5}{2}} \sqrt{x} \cot(2\pi x)\, \mathrm{cosec}(2\pi x) + \dfrac{\pi^{\frac{3}{2}}}{2\sqrt{x}} \mathrm{cosec}(2\pi x)$

(g) $(5\pi - 10\pi x \cot(2x - 5)) \csc(2x - 5)$

(h) $\dfrac{6 \sec(\pi x^3)(\pi x^3 \tan(\pi x^3) - 1)}{x^4}$

3. (a) $\dfrac{dy}{dx} = \dfrac{2 \sin x \cdot \cos x + \cot x \cdot \sin^2 x}{\csc x}$

(b) $\dfrac{dy}{dx} = \dfrac{-\pi x \cdot \csc^2(2\pi x) - \cot(2\pi x)}{2\pi x^3}$

(c) $\dfrac{dy}{dx} = 2 \cos(\cot x) \sin(\cot x) \csc^2 x$

(d) $\dfrac{dy}{dx} = -3 \sin^2(\sec x) \cos(\sec x) \tan x \sec x$

(e) $\dfrac{dy}{dx} = \dfrac{1}{\sin x - 1}$

(f) $\dfrac{dy}{dx} = \dfrac{\csc x}{\csc x - 1}$

(g) $\dfrac{dy}{dx} = 6(\sin(2x) - \cot(2x))^2(\cos(2x) + \csc^2(2x))$

(h) $\dfrac{dy}{dx} = \dfrac{2 \cos(x) + 4 + x \cdot \sin(x)}{(\cos(x) + 2)^{\frac{3}{2}}}$

(i) $\dfrac{dy}{dx} = \dfrac{x \cdot \sec^2(2x) - 2 \tan(2x) + 10}{x^3\sqrt{\tan(2x) - 5}}$

Chapter 3 Derivatives of Exponential and Logarithmic Functions

1. (a) $8e^{2x} + \dfrac{6x}{e^{x^2}}$

   (b) $8e^{\sec^2(4x)} \cdot \sec^2(4x) \cdot \tan(4x)$

   (c) $2xe^{x^2} \cdot \cos(e^{x^2}) + \dfrac{2\pi e^{\sqrt{2x}}}{\sqrt{2x}}$

   (d) $\dfrac{2}{x}$ (e) $\dfrac{1}{2x} - 10\cos(5x)\sin(5x)$

   (f) $\dfrac{-2\sin x \cos x + 4\pi}{\cos^2 x + 4\pi x}$

   (g) $xe^{\frac{x^2}{4}} + \dfrac{3}{x}$

   (h) $\dfrac{2\cos(2x)}{\sin(2x)}$

   (i) $5e^{-5x}\left(e^{10x}\cos(e^{5x}) + \operatorname{cosec}^2(e^{-5x})\right)$

2. (a) $f'(x) = \dfrac{-40e^{4x}}{(2e^{4x} + 3)^2}$

   (b) $f'(x) = 4x^2 e^{x^2}(2x^2 + 3)$

   (c) $f'(x) = 2\sin x \cos^3 x \cdot e^{\cos^2 x}$

(d) $f'(x) = -\dfrac{1}{2x(\ln(4x) + 3)^{\frac{3}{2}}}$

(e) $f'(x) = \dfrac{\cot^2 x}{2x} - 2\cot x \cdot \csc^2 x \,.\, \ln\sqrt{2x}$

(f) $f'(x) = -\sin\left(\dfrac{e^{4x}}{e^{3x-2}}\right)\left(\dfrac{e^{7x} - 8e^{4x}}{(e^{3x} - 2)^2}\right)$

(g) $f'(x) = \pi^2 \ln(\pi x)e^{\pi e^{\pi x} + \pi x} + \dfrac{e^{\pi e^{\pi x}}}{x}$

(h) $f'(x) = \dfrac{4x^2 e^{x^2} + 2e^{x^2} + \pi}{2\sqrt{2xe^{x^2} + \pi x}}$

(i) $\dfrac{\pi - 2\pi x^2 \ln(\pi x)}{xe^{x^2}}$

(j) $f'(x) = \dfrac{e^x + 4}{e^x + 4x} - \dfrac{e^{-x} + 4}{e^{-x} - 4x}$

3. (a) $\dfrac{dy}{dx} = \dfrac{e}{2x}$. When $x = 3$, $\dfrac{dy}{dx} = \dfrac{e}{6}$.

(b) $\dfrac{dy}{dx} = \dfrac{\sec(\ln(2x))\tan(\ln(2x))}{x}$.

When $x = 10$, $\dfrac{dy}{dx} = 5.24 \times 10^{-3}$.

(c) $\dfrac{dy}{d\theta} = e^{\sin\theta}\cos\theta - \dfrac{4\sin\theta}{\cos\theta}$.

When $\theta = 45°$, $\dfrac{dy}{d\theta} = -2.5659$.

(d) $f'(x) = \dfrac{-8e^{4x}}{(2e^{4x} + 3)^2}$. $f'(0) = -\dfrac{8}{25}$.

(e) $f'(x) = 2\ln(x) + 8xe^{4x^2} + 2$. $f'\left(\dfrac{1}{4}\right) = 1.795462$.

(f) $g'(\theta) = -4e\cos(\theta)\sin(\theta) + 2\cot\left(\dfrac{\theta}{2}\right)\csc\left(\dfrac{\theta}{2}\right)$.

$g'(30°) = 24.130872$.

> ## ◤ NOTE
>
> When using the calculator to evaluate cot, sec and cosec, first change the functions to $\cot x = \dfrac{1}{\tan x}$, $\sec x = \dfrac{1}{\cos x}$ and $\csc x = \dfrac{1}{\sin x}$ respectively. For e, change it to 2.718282.

Chapter 4 Implicit Differentiation

1. (a) $\dfrac{dy}{dx} = \dfrac{2 - y}{x - 3y}$

   (b) $\dfrac{dy}{dx} = \dfrac{2 - 3y^2}{6xy - 4}$

   (c) $\dfrac{dy}{dx} = \dfrac{150x^2 - y}{x + 50y}$

   (d) $\dfrac{dy}{dx} = \dfrac{y(3y - 2)}{2(x + 10y^6)}$

(e) $\dfrac{dy}{dx} = \dfrac{y(6x^2y + 1)}{x + 5y^3}$

(f) $\dfrac{dy}{dx} = \dfrac{y(-2xy^2 + 4y - 1)}{x^2y^2 - x + 3y^2}$

(g) $\dfrac{dy}{dx} = \dfrac{y^3(7x^6 + 3x^2 - 2y)}{2xy^3 + 5}$

(h) $\dfrac{dy}{dx} = \dfrac{y(12x^2y - 2y^3 - 1)}{x(4y^3 - 1)}$

2. (a) $\dfrac{dy}{dx} = \dfrac{\sqrt{y}\left(2e\pi\sqrt{5x} - 5\right)}{5\sqrt{x}}$

(b) $\dfrac{dy}{dx} = \dfrac{3x - 4\sin y}{4x\cos y + 2e\sin y}$

(c) $\dfrac{dy}{dx} = \dfrac{4e\pi\sqrt{y}\cos x}{1 - 16e\pi\sqrt{y}}$

(d) $\dfrac{dy}{dx} = \dfrac{y(\sin x - x\cos x)}{x(4xy^2\sin y - \sin x)}$

(e) $\dfrac{dy}{dx} = \dfrac{3(4y - \cos y)}{x(\sin y + 4)}$

(f) $\dfrac{dy}{dx} = \dfrac{xe^y\sin x - xy + 1}{x^2 + xe^y\cos x}$

(g) $\dfrac{dy}{dx} = \dfrac{y\cos^2 y(-8e^{4x} + 3\sin x)}{4y - 2\cos^2 y}$

3. (a) $\dfrac{dy}{dx} = \dfrac{-5y + 2}{5x + 2y}$; $\dfrac{dy}{dx}\Big|_{x=1,\, y=0} = \dfrac{2}{5}$

(b) $\dfrac{dy}{dx} = \dfrac{y(-10x + 1)}{5x^2 - x + 60y^2}$; $\dfrac{dy}{dx}\Big|_{x=2,\, y=-2} = \dfrac{19}{129}$

(c) $\dfrac{dy}{dx} = \dfrac{y(-3x^2 + 5)}{x(x^2 - 5)}$; $\dfrac{dy}{dx}\Big|_{x=1,\, y=1} = -\dfrac{1}{2}$

(d) $\dfrac{dy}{dx} = \dfrac{y(-5y^2 + 4y + 2)}{5xy^2 + 2x - 3y^4}$; $\dfrac{dy}{dx}\Big|_{x=3,\, y=-2} = \dfrac{26}{9}$

4. (a) $\dfrac{dy}{dx} = \dfrac{y^2(8x - 3y)}{3xy^2 - 1}$; $\dfrac{dy}{dx}\Big|_{(1,\,1)} = \dfrac{5}{2}$

(b) $\dfrac{dy}{dx} = \dfrac{2x - 3x^2}{5y^4 + 4y^3}$; $\dfrac{dy}{dx}\Big|_{(-1,\,1)} = -\dfrac{5}{9}$

(c) $\dfrac{dy}{dx} = -\dfrac{8x + y}{x - 6y}$; $\dfrac{dy}{dx}\Big|_{\left(1,\,\frac{4}{3}\right)} = \dfrac{4}{3}$

(d) $\dfrac{dy}{dx} = -\dfrac{9x^4 - 4x^2y + x + y}{x(4x^2 + 1)}$; $\dfrac{dy}{dx}\Big|_{(2,\,1)} = \dfrac{131}{34}$

Chapter 5   Partial Derivatives

1. (a) $\dfrac{\partial z}{\partial x} = 3x^2 - 6xy;$ (b) $\dfrac{\partial z}{\partial x} = \dfrac{2}{3y} + 8x;$

   $\dfrac{\partial z}{\partial y} = 8y - 3x^2$ $\dfrac{\partial z}{\partial y} = -\dfrac{2x}{3y^2} + \dfrac{12}{7}$

   (c) $\dfrac{\partial z}{\partial x} = \dfrac{y^2}{2\sqrt{x}} - 2x\sqrt{y} + \dfrac{2x}{y^2};$

   $\dfrac{\partial z}{\partial y} = 2y\sqrt{x} - \dfrac{x^2}{2\sqrt{y}} - \dfrac{2x^2}{y^3}$

   (d) $\dfrac{\partial z}{\partial x} = 24x^2 - 20y - 12xy^3;$

   $\dfrac{\partial z}{\partial y} = 60y^3 - 20x - 18x^2y^2$

   (e) $\dfrac{\partial z}{\partial x} = 24xy^2 - 48x^2 - 8y;$

   $\dfrac{\partial z}{\partial y} = 24x^2y + 18y^2 - 8x$

   (f) $\dfrac{\partial z}{\partial x} = \dfrac{26y}{(3y - 5x)^2};$

   $\dfrac{\partial z}{\partial y} = -\dfrac{26x}{(3y - 5x)^2}$

(g) $\dfrac{\partial z}{\partial x} = \dfrac{8x^2 + 32xy^2 + 4y^3}{(2x + 4y^2)^2}$;

$\dfrac{\partial z}{\partial y} = \dfrac{-12xy^2 - 32x^2y - 8y^4}{(2x + 4y^2)^2}$

(h) $\dfrac{\partial z}{\partial x} = 8x \cos(4x^2 - y^3)$;

$\dfrac{\partial z}{\partial y} = -3y^2 \cos(4x^2 - y^3)$

(i) $\dfrac{\partial z}{\partial x} = -\dfrac{5 \sin\left(\sqrt{5x} + \sqrt{3y}\right)}{2\sqrt{5x}}$;

$\dfrac{\partial z}{\partial y} = -\dfrac{3 \sin\left(\sqrt{5x} + \sqrt{3y}\right)}{2\sqrt{3y}}$

(j) $\dfrac{\partial z}{\partial x} = \dfrac{2x \cos(2x - 3y) - \sin(2x - 3y)}{3x^3y}$;

$\dfrac{\partial z}{\partial y} = -\dfrac{3y \cos(2x - 3y) + \sin(2x - 3y)}{3x^2y^2}$

2. (a) $\dfrac{\partial z}{\partial x} + \dfrac{\partial z}{\partial y} = 4e^{x^2-y^3}(2x - 3y^2)$

(b) $\dfrac{\partial z}{\partial x} + \dfrac{\partial z}{\partial y} = 2e^{2y}(2x + 1)$

(c) $\dfrac{\partial z}{\partial x} + \dfrac{\partial z}{\partial y} = \dfrac{12e^{4x}(\tan 4y - 4y \sec^2 4y)}{\tan^2 4y}$

4. (a) $x\dfrac{\partial V}{\partial x} + z\dfrac{\partial V}{\partial z} = -\dfrac{3y^3}{z^3} f'\left(\dfrac{x^3 + y^3}{z^3}\right)$

(b) $2y\dfrac{\partial V}{\partial y} - 2z\dfrac{\partial V}{\partial z} = \left(\sqrt{2y} - \sqrt{2z}\right) f'\left(\sqrt{2x} + \sqrt{2y} + \sqrt{2z}\right)$

(c) $\sqrt{2x}\,\dfrac{\partial V}{\partial x} + \dfrac{1}{y}\dfrac{\partial V}{\partial y} + z\dfrac{\partial V}{\partial z}$

$= \left(\dfrac{3\sqrt{2x} + 9y^2 + 7}{z^3}\right) f'\left(\dfrac{\sqrt{2x} + 3y^2}{z^3}\right)$

5. (a) $\dfrac{\partial z}{\partial r} = 12(2x^2 - sy^3); \dfrac{\partial z}{\partial s} = 12(4x^2 - ry^3)$

(b) $\dfrac{\partial z}{\partial x} = (16r - 16s)(2x - y^2); \dfrac{\partial z}{\partial y} = (32ry - 32sy)(1 - x)$

(c) $\dfrac{\partial z}{\partial r} = 2r\{(8x + 2)\cos\theta + (6y + 1)\sin\theta\};$

$\dfrac{\partial z}{\partial \theta} = r^2\{(6y + 1)\cos\theta - (8x + 2)\sin\theta\}$

APPENDIX

To differentiate $f(x) = \cos(x)$ from first principles:

Let h be a small increment in the value of x.

Then, $f(x + h) = \cos(x + h)$

Thus, $f'(x) = \lim\limits_{h \to 0} \dfrac{f(x + h) - f(x)}{h}$

$= \lim\limits_{h \to 0} \dfrac{\cos(x + h) - \cos(x)}{h}$

$= \lim\limits_{h \to 0} \dfrac{\cos(x)\cos(h) - \sin(x)\sin(h) - \cos(x)}{h}$

└─┤ Apply Sum–Difference formula

$= \lim\limits_{h \to 0} \dfrac{\cos(x)\cos(h) - \cos(x) - \sin(x)\sin(h)}{h}$

$= \lim\limits_{h \to 0} \dfrac{\cos(x)\cos(h) - \cos(x)}{h} - \lim\limits_{h \to 0} \dfrac{\sin(x)\sin(h)}{h}$

$= \lim\limits_{h \to 0} \dfrac{\cos(x)(\cos(h) - 1)}{h} - \lim\limits_{h \to 0} \dfrac{\sin(x)\sin(h)}{h}$

└─┤ Extract the common factor $\cos(x)$

$$= \cos(x) \lim_{h \to 0} \frac{(\cos(h) - 1)}{h} - \sin(x) \lim_{h \to 0} \frac{\sin(h)}{h}$$

$$= \cos(x) \cdot 0 - \sin(x) \cdot 1$$

$$= \mathbf{-sin(x)}$$

Refer to page 32

FURTHER READING

Ahmad, S., Ramli, N., and Mohamed Nor, A. H. (2013). *Basic Calculus: For Science and Engineering Students.* JAPENA Universiti Teknologi Mara Pahang (Malaysia).

Cheng, S. P., Teoh, S. H., and Ng, S. F. (2008). *Mathematics for Matriculation 2*, 3rd Edition. Oriental Academic Publication.

How, G. A. and Ong, B. H. (2007). *Calculus.* Penerbit Universiti Sains Malaysia.

Lynch, B. J., Andrews, L. E., and Keating, H. M. (1985). *Mathematics A Year 12.* Longman.

Nykamp, D. Q. (2014). "Partial derivative examples". From *Math Insight*, http://mathinsight.org/partial_derivative_examples

Rehill, G. S. and McAuliffe, R. (1999). *Mathematical Methods Units 3 & 4*, 3rd Edition. Macmillan.

Sheikh Abdullah, S. A., Ch'ng, P. E., Teoh, S. H., Hamat, M., and Abdul Razak, N. A. (2009). *First Engineering Mathematics*, 3rd Edition. McGraw-Hill (Malaysia).

Tan, S. T. (2010). *Applied Mathematics for the Managerial, Life, and Social Sciences*, 5th Edition. Cengage Learning.

Weisstein, E. W. (2014). "Implicit differentiation". From *MathWorld* — *A Wolfram Web Resource*, http://mathworld.wolfram.com/ ImplicitDifferentiation.html